101 Ways to Become a

Superhero

. . . Or an Evil Genius

Dedicated to

Marlie and Kitty *

* Write your own dedication here

Did you use
this book for . . .

GOOD? or

☐

EVIL?

☒

Originally published in Great Britain by Bloomsbury Publishing Plc in 2010
First published in the United States of America in April 2011
by Walker Publishing Company, Inc., a division of Bloomsbury Publishing, Inc.
www.bloomsburyteens.com

For information about permission to reproduce selections from this book, write to
Permissions, Walker BFYR, 175 Fifth Avenue, New York, New York 10010

Library of Congress Cataloging-in-Publication Data
Horne, Richard.
101 ways to become a superhero . . . or an evil genius /
by Richard Horne and Helen Szirtes ; illustrated by Richard Horne.
p.   cm.
ISBN 978-0-8027-2171-6
1. Conduct of life—Juvenile literature. 2. Life skills—Juvenile literature. I. Szirtes, Helen. II. Horne,
Richard, ill. III. Title. IV. Title: One hundred and one ways to become a superhero . . . or an evil genius.
BJ1631.H67 2011   646.7—dc22   2010008447

Printed in Malaysia by Tien Wah Press, Johor Bahru, Johor
2 4 6 8 10 9 7 5 3 1

All papers used by Bloomsbury Publishing, Inc., are natural, recyclable products
made from wood grown in well-managed forests. The manufacturing processes
conform to the environmental regulations of the country of origin.

101 Ways to Become a

Superhero

... Or an Evil Genius

Written by Helen Szirtes and Richard Horne
Designed and illustrated by Richard Horne

Walker & Company
New York

Introduction

Well done. You have passed the test. Since you have a copy of this book in your hands, you must have sensed your potential for greatness, or someone else has seen it in you and is giving you the nudge you need to develop those extraordinary abilities. Recognizing that you're destined to be one of the few and accepting the dark and lonely path that comes with the responsibility of wielding such awesome superpowers is always a bittersweet moment.

Master

You will have to use every last drop of physical and mental energy you have to attain the levels of skill required in your future role as superhero, or, for the more criminally minded, evil genius.

Complete

Keep track of your superhuman feats by filling in the easy-to-follow forms.

Kick Ass

Only when you have mastered all the superpowers in this book; committed to memory all the advice it has to offer; and equipped yourself with the right look, tools, and support for the monumental challenges that lie ahead are you ready to engage with the final part of the test: kicking ass.

How to Use This Book

The idea is simple. Master or complete the **101 Ways to Become a Superhero**, check the boxes, fill in the forms, and stick in the colored stars as you go.

About the Forms

- Be honest with the information you enter in the forms. Only evil geniuses are allowed to lie about their achievements.
- There may be a few tricky questions on some of the forms. Don't worry if you get stuck—you'll find the answers at the back of the book.
- You may find some of the forms too small for all the information you'd like to enter. To solve this problem you can copy and use the extra pages at the back of the book or visit the website for extra or duplicate pages at **www.101thingstodobook.com**.

Your Super **Ways to Become a Superhero**

If there are superpowers you'd like to master that aren't mentioned in the book, add your top ten **Ways to Become a Superhero** on the pages provided at the back.

Helpful Tips

The tips on the opposite page offer some guidelines to completing the **Ways to Become a Superhero**.

101 Ways to Become
a Superhero . . . Or an Evil Genius

Tips

- ☑ Be patient. Becoming a superhero or villain requires a lot of work and dedication.

- ☑ Take small steps. You have to walk before you can fly, but by beginning your training young, you will stay a step ahead of your rivals.

- ☑ Always carry this book with you, as opportunities to practice your superpowers may present themselves at unexpected moments.

- ☑ Some superpowers cannot be accomplished without a little courage. But don't do anything beyond your current capabilities if you think it may be dangerous.

- ☑ Be creative. Unless you were born with special abilities, it may take a bit of ingenuity to complete some of the tasks.

- ☑ You don't have to do it alone. Your sidekick or superteam can assist you with much of this training— and make it even more enjoyable.

- ☑ If at first you don't succeed, keep trying. Some superpowers will take many attempts and lots of practice to accomplish.

- ☑ Don't procrastinate. Fill out the form as soon as you've accomplished a task or superpower, before you forget the details.

- ☑ Push yourself. Do things you would normally avoid doing.

- ☑ Above all, have fun!

101 Ways to Become
a Superhero . . . Or an Evil Genius

Some Things You Will Need

Here is a list of some of the items that will come in handy as you complete the **101 Ways to Become a Superhero . . . Or an Evil Genius**. You don't need to gather them all before you start, but it's advisable to at least have a pen, a pair of scissors, glue, a camera, access to a computer, and some money. You can pick up the other things as you progress through the list, but the willingness to learn, a sense of adventure, spontaneity, a dark sense of humor, ingenious cunning, and a spectacular imagination are all essential.

- ☐ A secret hiding place for this book!
- ☐ A pen
- ☐ A pair of scissors
- ☐ Glue
- ☐ A camera
- ☐ A computer
- ☐ Some money
- ☐ A photocopier
- ☐ Cooperative family and friends
- ☐ Boundless courage
- ☐ Determination
- ☐ Patience
- ☐ A head for heights
- ☐ A need for speed
- ☐ Confidence
- ☐ Various animals
- ☐ Sewing skills
- ☐ A daredevil spirit
- ☐ Fabrics
- ☐ Cardboard
- ☐ A flashlight
- ☐ A cell phone
- ☐ A silver tongue
- ☐ Earth, wind, air, and fire
- ☐ Darkness
- ☐ Physical prowess
- ☐ Mental mastery
- ☐ Keen intuition
- ☐ Plexiglas
- ☐ Balloons
- ☐ Zombies
- ☐ A nemesis
- ☐ A sidekick or henchmen
- ☐ A thirst for knowledge
- ☐ Honorable or dishonorable intentions
- ☐ Moral uprightness or depravity
- ☐ Beanbags
- ☐ Tennis balls
- ☐ Access to outside open space
- ☐ Robots
- ☐ A swimsuit
- ☐ Paints
- ☐ Self-discipline
- ☐ A stopwatch
- ☐ Baked beans
- ☐ A mask
- ☐ A world map
- ☐ A chair
- ☐ Smelly things
- ☐ Paper clips
- ☐ An invisibility cloak
- ☐ A manifesto
- ☐ A secret code
- ☐ A thermometer
- ☐ The sun
- ☐ A secret base
- ☐ Sponges
- ☐ A variety pack of cereals
- ☐ Great coordination
- ☐ A bike
- ☐ Useful contacts
- ☐ Acting skills

101 Ways to Become
a Superhero . . . Or an Evil Genius

Important Information

WARNING:

WHEN EMBARKING ON THE 101 WAYS TO BECOME A SUPERHERO . . . OR AN EVIL GENIUS PLEASE PROCEED WITH CARE.

FOR SOME OF THE ACTIVITIES YOU WILL NEED THE **SUPER**VISION OF A **SUPER**ADULT. IF IN DOUBT, CONSULT AN ADULT ANYWAY.

THE AUTHORS AND PUBLISHER ACCEPT NO RESPONSIBILITY FOR ANY ACCIDENTS THAT OCCUR AS A RESULT OF USING THIS BOOK.

101 Ways to Become
a Superhero . . . Or an Evil Genius

The List

1. ☐ Discover Your Alter Ego
2. ☐ Choose Your Name
3. ☐ Take Flight
4. ☐ Have a Twisted Backstory
5. ☐ Super-Vision
6. ☐ Stamina
7. ☐ Decipher Devious Riddles
8. ☐ Kick Ass Humanely
9. ☐ Select a Sidekick
10. ☐ Stealth
11. ☐ Groom Your Dark Side
12. ☐ Mind Control
13. ☐ Conquer Your Fears
14. ☐ Strength
15. ☐ Save the World from Rampaging Robots
16. ☐ Sixth Sense
17. ☐ Choose Your Outfit
18. ☐ Harness the Elements
19. ☐ Know Whom to Save First
20. ☐ Learn to Multitask
21. ☐ Dexterity
22. ☐ Communicate with Animals
23. ☐ Plan for World Domination
24. ☐ Design a Logo
25. ☐ Control Your Temper
26. ☐ Know Your Weaknesses
27. ☐ See in the Dark
28. ☐ Balance
29. ☐ Solve Impossible Problems
30. ☐ Save the World from Alien Attack
31. ☐ Identify Your Nemesis
32. ☐ Get a Villainous Chair
33. ☐ Anticipate Your Enemy's Next Move
34. ☐ Supersmell
35. ☐ Identify Opportunities to Help
36. ☐ Be in Two Places at Once
37. ☐ Train Your Superpet
38. ☐ Assemble Your Armies of Darkness
39. ☐ Speed
40. ☐ Understand Body Language
41. ☐ Become a Science Genius
42. ☐ Strike a Superhero Pose
43. ☐ Invisibility
44. ☐ Never Give Up
45. ☐ Save the World from Scary Monsters
46. ☐ Choose a Cause
47. ☐ Master of Illusion
48. ☐ Choose a Calling Card
49. ☐ Hone Your Moral Compass
50. ☐ Second Sight
51. ☐ Jump High
52. ☐ Telekinesis
53. ☐ Be Ruthless
54. ☐ Make Sacrifices
55. ☐ Break Codes

101 Ways to Become
a Superhero . . . Or an Evil Genius

The List

56. ☐ Invent Some Great One-Liners
57. ☐ Photographic Memory
58. ☐ Withstand Heat and Cold
59. ☐ Take Risks
60. ☐ Save the World from the Undead
61. ☐ Locate Your Secret Base
62. ☐ Superhearing
63. ☐ Observation Skills
64. ☐ Travel in Time
65. ☐ Talk Your Way Out of Trouble
66. ☐ Agility
67. ☐ Select a Call Signal
68. ☐ Survive Your Fatal Flaw
69. ☐ Kung-Fu Master
70. ☐ Cope Under Pressure
71. ☐ Trace Your Superhero Origins
72. ☐ Speak a Hundred Languages
73. ☐ Create a Force Field
74. ☐ Identify and Interpret Clues
75. ☐ Save the World from Environmental Disaster
76. ☐ Devise an Escape Plan
77. ☐ X-Ray Vision
78. ☐ Be a Good Influence
79. ☐ Design Your Own Gadgets
80. ☐ Orientation
81. ☐ Make the Right Decisions—Fast
82. ☐ Get a Head for Business
83. ☐ Hand–Eye Skill
84. ☐ Resist Temptation
85. ☐ Shape-Shift
86. ☐ Keep Supersecrets
87. ☐ Interrogation
88. ☐ Acquire Specialist Knowledge
89. ☐ Know When Someone's Lying
90. ☐ Healing
91. ☐ Design Your Supertransport
92. ☐ Telepathy
93. ☐ Develop Powers of Persuasion
94. ☐ Talk to Computers
95. ☐ Build a Network of Contacts
96. ☐ Lead from the Front
97. ☐ Know What's Happening Everywhere
98. ☐ Swim Like a Fish
99. ☐ Gather a Superteam
100. ☐ Devise Your Villainous Comeback
101. ☐ Save the World from Yourself

Discover Your Alter Ego

Your alter ego is your worst enemy and your best friend. You live together but you cannot be in each other's company. You don't have much in common and yet you share an existence. To be a superhero or a supervillain, it is fundamental that you discover your alter ego, that you allow it space to develop but that you never ever let on that you have it.

Two-Faced

- Have you ever had a love-hate relationship with something or someone? This is a good indication of your alter ego making its presence felt. In these cases, do you predominantly end up going with the instinctive option or the sensible one? Whichever you do, start to indulge the other side more often.
- One way to coax your alter ego out of its shell is to try doing things you wouldn't normally dream of doing. For example, if you hate walking, climbing a mountain is probably not something you're desperate to do, but give it a try and listen to the inner voice for signs of enjoyment.
- He or she may be your other half, but this relationship with your alter ego is hardly a marriage made in heaven—nor should you try to make it so. On the contrary, never compromise with it. Be you, or be your alter ego. Don't try to be some crazy mix of the two. It won't work. If your idea of fun is reading a book while your alter ego yearns to go on some hair-raising roller-coaster ride, don't think you can satisfy your other half by reading a book about roller coasters.

A Jekyll and Hyde warning: Mr. Hyde had to kill himself off when he realized he couldn't go back to being Dr. Jekyll. Don't unleash your alter ego unless you know how to control him/her. Find his/her off button or your secret identity won't be the only thing at risk.

Discover Your Alter Ego **Form**

Once you have mastered this **Way to Become a Superhero**,
stick your Achieved Star here and fill in the form

☆ **Achieved**

TWO'S COMPANY

Monitor your thoughts, feelings, and behavior for a week to get a picture of the balance of power
between you and your alter ego. Record your findings below.

% 100 %

YOU
List up to ten of your own
characteristics

1. loves cats
2. Plays xbox
3.
4.
5.
6.
7.
8.
9.
10.

90

80

70

60

50

40

30

20

% 10 %

ALTER EGO
List up to ten of your alter ego's
characteristics

1.
2.
3.
4.
5.
6.
7.
8.
9.
10.

Color in the figure above to show what percentage of your behavior is controlled by you and what
percentage is controlled by your alter ego. Use green for you and red for your alter ego.

Who is the more dominant character?   You ☐   Your alter ego ☐

Did you use this power for....

If it's you, what can you do to coax
your alter ego out of his/her shell?

If it's your alter ego, what can you do to
rein him/her in and assert control?

GOOD? or

☐ **EVIL?** ☒

At the same time you could master these other **Ways**:
11: Groom Your Dark Side • **25**: Control Your Temper • **26**: Know Your Weaknesses
31: Identify Your Nemesis • **86**: Keep Supersecrets • **101**: Save the World from Yourself

Copy and cut out the name badge above and award yourself 1–5 gold stars from the back of the book, depending on how good a superhero you think you are.

Choose Your Name

"What's in a name?" said Shakespeare's Juliet from her balcony. But what did she know? She died soon after that. For a superhero or villain, your name is your identity: it tells the world who you are and what you do. Your name will take on legendary status. It might even become a successful brand. So choose a memorable one with mystique, power, and authority.

World Title

- Start by making a list of words that sum up your best parts. If you have a superpower that is your trademark, think of a term that encapsulates it.
- Look to your past for inspiration. Perhaps you discovered your superhuman abilities in a radioactive bog. So you could call yourself Gunk-Girl or the Drip. Or something more glamorous. Slimeshifter, perhaps?
- Some superheroes and villains prefer a title, like Doctor, Captain, Lady, or Mr. Others affix a simple -Man, -Woman, -Boy, or -Girl to the end of their name.
- You could incorporate a color, but make sure it suits you.
- Look to the worlds of folklore and magic for inspiration, or science and nature if that's more your thing. Are you like an ancient god (e.g., Thoth, Egyptian god of secrets)? An animal (e.g., Hammerhead)? A force of nature (e.g., Tornado)? A scientific phenomenon (e.g., Fusion)?
- It's not easy to sum up what you do in a word. Another method is to follow the pattern Name + the + Thing, like Howard the Duck or Conan the Barbarian. But don't overdo the detail (e.g., Astronorty the Star Rider Who Can Travel Light-Years in Mere Seconds).

Think outside the box: Feel free to adapt words or make them up. Adding suffixes is a good trick (e.g., Graviton, Velociter) and puns can be great (e.g., the Thundertaker, the Crime Minister). Try tweaking the spelling of a word to make it look more like a name (e.g., Flyte).

Choose Your Name **Form**

Once you have mastered this **Way to Become a Superhero**, stick your Achieved Star here and fill in the form

Achieved

SUPER WHO?

Finding a name that completely sums you up can be really tough. The questions below will help you to focus on the task and generate some ideas that may lead you to your final supername.

What are your top three superpowers?

Who is your superhero inspiration?

IF YOU WERE . . .
. . . an animal, what animal would you be?

What is your nickname, if you have one?

. . . a force of nature, what kind would you be?

What do you wish your parents had named you?

. . . a color, what color would you be?

What is the name of your favorite character from a book/movie?

. . . a scientific phenomenon, what kind would you be?

DID YOU TRY YOUR NAME WITH . . .   . . . "The" in front?   y/n

. . . Man/Boy/Girl/Woman after it?   y/n

. . . a title in front of it (e.g., Captain)?   y/n

If yes, which title worked best?

WRITE YOUR SUPERNAME HERE

Did you use this power for . . .
GOOD? or **EVIL?**

Once you've made your choice, you can start working on a logo. In the meantime, write your new supername on the outfit above.

At the same time you could master these other **Ways**:
4: Have a Twisted Backstory • **17**: Choose Your Outfit • **42**: Strike a Superhero Pose
56: Invent Some Great One-Liners • **71**: Trace Your Superhero Origins

Take Flight

If you've ever dreamed you're flying, it's a good sign that the secret to this special power lies deep within you. Humans evolved from apes, and while you don't see many flying monkeys (unless they're in the service of wicked witches), all those years leaping from tree to tree came pretty close to flying. To reconnect with this power, reach back into your evolutionary past. Way back. Back to the time before creatures crawled out of the sea onto land . . .

For Your Eyes Only

- The best place to develop the skills required for flight is, strange as it may seem, in the swimming pool, where the water offers you a weightlessness and freedom of movement that we land-bound creatures get precious little of. In the water you can practice gliding and floating—two essentials of effortless flight. It will also give you the valuable experience of harnessing currents—in this case water, but later it could be air!
- The other thing to practice at the swimming pool is diving. Start small (off the side of the pool) and, with the right professional instruction, you can work your way up, up, and up, to the highest diving boards. Who knows? One day you might launch off and find your journey down much slower and more controlled than you expected.
- As you progress, you may want to set yourself the challenge of learning some tricks on a trampoline. The most basic is the tuck jump, where you bring your arms down and tuck your knees underneath. Or try touching your toes when you're up in the air!

Join the jet set: If natural flight doesn't suit your style, you could look at a jet pack. The first "rocket belt" was invented in 1961 by Wendell Moore, but there's been little advance in the technology since his death. The main problem was the flight time—only 25 seconds.

Take Flight **Form**

Once you have mastered this **Way to Become a Superhero**, stick your Achieved Star here and fill in the form

Achieved

———— FLYING SHAME ————

The person who said the camera never lies couldn't have been more wrong. Whether you use the timer to snap yourself midleap, tamper with your photos on a computer, or paint a backdrop and lie on top of it in a Superman pose while your sidekick photographs you from above, there are always ways to fake flying while you figure out how to do it for real.

Who took the photo?

How did you fake the flying?

Rate the fake

| Will only fool fools | y/n | Will fool some people | y/n |
| Will fool everyone | y/n | It's not a fake —I flew | y/n |

Place a photo of you flying here

Who took the photo?

How did you fake the flying?

Rate the fake

Will fool everyone | y/n

Will fool some people | y/n

Will only fool fools | y/n

It's not a fake —I flew | y/n

Place a photo of you flying here

Did you use this power for...

GOOD? *or*

☐ **EVIL?**

☐

At the same time you could master these other **Ways**:
13: Conquer Your Fears • **22**: Communicate with Animals • **41**: Become a Science Genius • **47**: Master of Illusion • **51**: Jump High • **80**: Orientation • **98**: Swim Like a Fish

IT STARTED WITH A *THUNDERSTORM* . . .

Have a Twisted Backstory

Ask any psychologist and they'll tell you we all grow up to be products of our environment and our childhood experiences. Knowing the backstory to your evil ways will help you to understand your motives and form the basis for believing in what you do, even if everyone else tells you it's fiendish and depraved. So, if you don't have one, start inventing one now. It's part of who you are.

Hard Knock Life

- Look back over your life. Has anything happened to you that stands out as being particularly significant, proving to be a turning point at which you realized you were destined to be one of life's bad guys?
- Examine your motives for clues. If you're driven by revenge, who are you targeting and why? If it's power you want, have you been cruelly deprived of it before? Do your evil aims or methods suggest you're trying to make a point or spitting a bitter taste out of your mouth?
- Perhaps you've lived a charmed life and have never endured hardship or been the victim of injustice. Could it be that you just felt an urge to redress the balance in your life, to rebel against all the suffocating love you've been shown? Having been spoiled rotten, do you now find that you always have to get your own way?
- If your backstory's still a mystery, you may be blocking out painful memories, such as being abandoned as a baby and raised by evil squirrels. Or perhaps you were abducted by aliens and brainwashed.

Reasons to be hateful: Here are some motives for you to consider: envy, hate, insecurity, paranoia, power, revenge, greed, insanity, and evil for evil's sake (i.e., fun). What is at the root of your motives? If you can discover that, you'll find the backstory to your pain.

Have a Twisted Backstory **Form**

Once you have mastered this **Way to Become an Evil Genius**, stick your Achieved Star here and fill in the form

Achieved

How did you get to be so evil and twisted?
Fill out the psychological profile below.

Don't forget to add some deranged doodles to decorate your form.

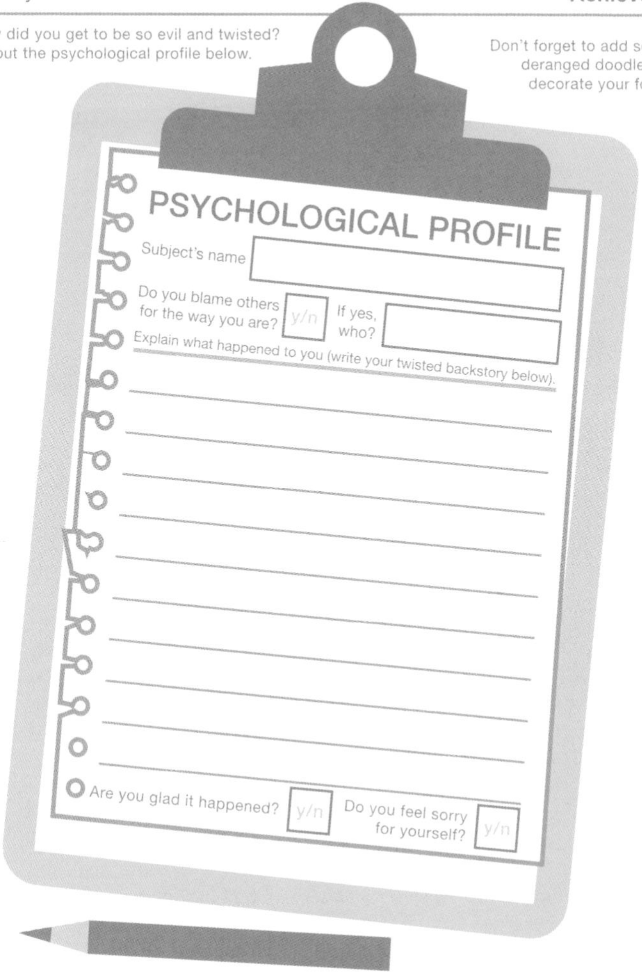

PSYCHOLOGICAL PROFILE

Subject's name

Do you blame others for the way you are? [y/n]   If yes, who?

Explain what happened to you (write your twisted backstory below).

Are you glad it happened? [y/n]   Do you feel sorry for yourself? [y/n]

At the same time you could master these other **Ways**:
1: Discover Your Alter Ego • **11**: Groom Your Dark Side • **31**: Identify Your Nemesis
46: Choose a Cause • **68**: Survive Your Fatal Flaw • **71**: Trace Your Superhero Origins

Super-Vision

Seeing is believing, and if you can't see the forest for the trees, you're being short-sighted about what's required of a superhero. Turn those peepers into telescopic lenses so that you can see trouble coming a mile away and are ready to face it.

Out of Sight

- In China it is common in schools and factories to do eye exercises. Start by moving your eyes from side to side, then around in circles clockwise and counterclockwise. You can do eye massage too, but you must be very gentle so you don't hurt yourself. Massage your temples, moving your fingers in a circular motion, first clockwise, then counterclockwise. You can also do the area just below the outside corners of your eyes and rub the bridge of your nose, and very gently stroke across your closed eyelids, from inner to outer edge.
- Look at objects close up, mid-distance, and far away, and see how quickly your eyes can adjust and refocus. You can also try holding a pencil at arm's length and slowly bringing it toward your nose, following it with your eyes all the time.
- Peripheral vision is important too, so ask your sidekick to pick up an object and stand behind you, then slowly move around in an arc to the front while you focus on looking straight ahead. At what point can you see what your sidekick is holding out of the corner of your eye? Is it the same for both eyes?

Blind as a bat: If you're a bespectacled superbeing in the making, don't worry. Think about bats. They get around just fine without being able to see a thing. Let your ears be your eyes, and get working hard on developing your superhearing to make up for it.

Super-Vision Form

Once you have mastered this **Way to Become a Superhero**, stick your Achieved Star here and fill in the form

Achieved

SEE SURE

Ask your sidekick to hold up this page while you try to read each line of letters from a few feet away. Try again, moving farther away each time, until you can no longer read the last line.

1 S

2 U P

3 E R H

4 E R O E

5 S C A N S

6 P Y E V I L G E N

7 I U S E S F R O M

8 A L O N G W A Y O F F

What's the maximum distance you can read the bottom line? `0 0` ft `0 0` in

Try the test again in a darkened room.

What distance did you manage this time? `0 0` ft `0 0` in

SEE SIDE

With your sidekick's help, you can put your peripheral vision to the test. Focus on a point directly in front of you while your sidekick, holding a mystery object, moves slowly in an arc from behind you around to your front. On the diagram below, mark the spot on your right, then on your left, when you were able to see what your sidekick was holding. Keep looking straight ahead!

Attempt 1

RIGHT

Attempt 2

LEFT

What was your sidekick holding?

Attempt 1

Attempt 2

Did you use this power for...

GOOD? or

EVIL?

Which side was your peripheral vision best?   Left ☐   Right ☐

At the same time you could master these other **Ways**:
16: Sixth Sense • **27**: See in the Dark • **34**: Supersmell • **62**: Superhearing
63: Observation Skills • **77**: X-Ray Vision

Stamina

Are you a sprinter or a long-distance runner? Most people find they are better suited to one than the other, but as a superhero you must excel at both. Some tasks require extended periods of huge effort, such as a long chase, rescuing people one by one from a burning building, or carrying an attractive stranger's shopping bags up ten flights of stairs. Stamina is about using your energy in a way that enables you to put in consistent effort for longer.

The Long Haul

- The key with exercise is to build it up slowly to avoid injury and to work it into your daily routine. Next time you need to go down or up the stairs, do it twice before continuing. The following time, do it three times, and then four—and so on.
- Aerobic exercise is vital. It strengthens the muscles around the heart and increases lung capacity, allowing a faster supply of oxygen to the rest of the body. Jumping rope, running, swimming, and cycling are all good stamina-building activities. Choose something you enjoy and build up the distance/duration of your training gradually. You need to push yourself, but not over your limits, so include good rest or recovery periods if you need to. For example, you could do two minutes of fast jump rope followed by three minutes of steady running in place.
- After about six months of regular training, you should be ready to tackle a fun run or marathon. If you love swimming and cycling too, make it the ultimate endurance test—a triathlon.

Eat well and regularly: Snack to help keep energy levels up—but not on chips and chocolate! You want carbohydrate-rich foods, but those with the sort of energy the body can release slowly, like bananas, whole-grain cereals, and whole wheat bread and pasta.

Stamina Form

Once you have mastered this **Way to Become a Superhero**, stick your Achieved Star here and fill in the form

Achieved

— WORK IT OUT —

To be "super" you need to be superfit, and this means a lot of training. Over the course of four weeks, monitor your progress by putting your long-distance stamina to the test with the following challenges. Each week you should aim to smash the previous week's record.

Exercise 1 — Run as far as you can without stopping.

Week 1	Week 2	Week 3	Week 4
0 0 0 0 mi	0 0 0 0 mi	0 0 0 0 mi	0 0 0 0 mi

Exercise 2 — Swim as far as you can without stopping.

Week 1	Week 2	Week 3	Week 4
0 0 0 laps	0 0 0 laps	0 0 0 laps	0 0 0 laps

Exercise 3 — Cycle uphill as far as you can without stopping.

Week 1	Week 2	Week 3	Week 4
0 0 0 0 mi	0 0 0 0 mi	0 0 0 0 mi	0 0 0 0 mi

Exercise 4 — Attempt as many sit-ups as you can.

Week 2: 0 0 0
Week 3: 0 0 0
Week 1: 0 0 0
Week 4: 0 0 0

Exercise 5 — Jump rope as many times as you can.

Week 2: 0 0 0
Week 3: 0 0 0
Week 1: 0 0 0
Week 4: 0 0 0

Did you use this power for... **GOOD?** or ☐ **EVIL?** ☐

At the same time you could master these other **Ways:**
14: Strength • **39**: Speed • **44**: Never Give Up • **70**: Cope Under Pressure
87: Interrogation

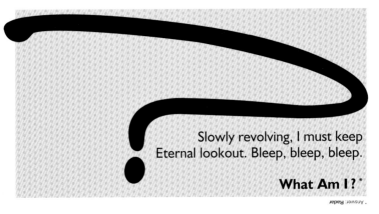

Slowly revolving, I must keep
Eternal lookout. Bleep, bleep, bleep.

What Am I? *

* Answer: Radar

Decipher Devious Riddles

Evil geniuses love to pit their wits against their enemies' by giving them some devilish challenges. More often than not, these will include a series of riddles with diabolical consequences for wrong answers.

Talking in Riddles

- Like poetry, riddles often rely on imagery. "What goes on four legs in the morning, two legs at noon, and three legs in the evening?" In this famous riddle from Greek mythology, the key is to identify the metaphors being used. What else might those time markers signify?

- Another type of riddle is the conundrum, which uses word play to mislead and delight. "When is a door not a door?" is a good example of this type. The pun is in the answer, not the question.

- When faced with a riddle, break it down into chunks. As well as possible metaphors, look for homonyms (words with more than one meaning, like "stalk") and homophones (words that sound the same but are spelled differently, like "horse" and "hoarse"). Don't be hasty in drawing any conclusions. Words that you usually associate with one thing may be used in a less obvious way (e.g., "face"—we think of a human one first, but a clock has a face too).

- Study cryptic crosswords. The clues look like nonsense, but they're basically riddles and employ a similar kind of code. Part of the code might be a phrase telling you the answer is in the clue itself (e.g., phrases like "turn around" or "mix up" might point to an anagram).

Riddle me this: Another great way to become a riddle master is to start writing riddles yourself: that way, you enter the mind-set of the riddler and learn to think about how to phrase things in misleading (but accurate) ways. Devise some for your sidekick to solve.

Decipher Devious Riddles **Form**

Once you have mastered this **Way to Become a Superhero**,
stick your Achieved Star here and fill in the form

Achieved

RIDDLE-ME-REE

Time to test your riddle-deciphering abilities. All the answers are at the back of the book.
Here's an easy one to get you started. You even get a clue: think superhero.

1.
King of the worldwide web
Swinging between the tower blocks of the city.
When dawn arrives, the street's wrapped up.
Crime-fighting can be pretty.

WHO AM I?

After that gentle introduction, you'll be ready for some more
challenging riddles. All the clues you need are in this book.

2.
Farsighted? Nearsighted? Through-sighted, me!
Whatever you are is fully illustrated.
No use hiding. No use dressing up.
Your lies are transparent, your plots laid bare, X-rated.

WHAT AM I?

3.
You might have started thinking I'm your friend
But how things start are not quite how they end.
And so we meet at last, here in the very place
You wouldn't expect to see my half-familiar face.
But all the time you knew we'd have to meet.
My work is about to begin. Please take a seat.

WHO AM I?

4.
Wherever you have been, I am left behind.
I am your maze, your winding path, your self.
You steal the book but I stay on the shelf
For anyone to find.
The truth, as ever, makes a pretty sum,
My very being lies under your thumb,
My face, though new, already deeply lined.

WHAT AM I?

RIDDLE-YOU-REE

Now it's your turn to try
being the riddler. What will
you choose for your subject?
A person, an object, a
superpower, an emotion?
When you've finished, try it
out on your sidekick.

Could they see through
your deviousness?

y/n

*Did you use
this power for....*

GOOD? *or*

☐ **EVIL?**

☐

At the same time you could master these other **Ways**:
29: Solve Impossible Problems • **55**: Break Codes • **56**: Invent Some Great
One-Liners • **72**: Speak a Hundred Languages • **74**: Identify and Interpret Clues

Kick Ass Humanely

Just because your nemesis insults your mother, steals your girl, and laughs in your face doesn't mean you have to serve him a knuckle sandwich. And just because aliens want to suck out everyone's brains, yours included, doesn't mean you need to start an intergalactic war. In other words, you may be able to kick some serious ass, but that doesn't always mean you should.

Why Can't We All Just Get Along?

- Using force is one option, but preferably only as a backup. What are the other options? Devise a way to catch your rat and dispose of it without breaking its neck and making its eyes pop out—it's called a humane trap. Practice on your sidekick. The element of surprise can be your best weapon if you're trying to . . . well, avoid using weapons.
- You must learn self-defense and disarming maneuvers if you're going to be an agent of peace and justice. Ask your sidekick to help you train by arming them with a dummy weapon and trying to neutralize them before they use it on you (or someone else). You'll need to provide them with protective gear, since you won't always be able to guarantee that your humane methods are quite humane enough.
- Focus on improving your aim, so that you can knock something out of someone's hand from a distance. Also look at more subtle ways of distracting and disabling your enemy. It might be through noises, by making them itch or laugh or sneeze, by blinding or disorienting them— anything that isn't going to inflict long-term damage.

Let's talk about it: No one likes confrontation (head straight to the Supervillainous section if you do), but mad, bad types can be hard to reason with. Practice your diplomacy skills by intervening in arguments and trying to stop them from getting out of hand.

Kick Ass Humanely **Form**

Once you have mastered this **Way to Become a Superhero**,
stick your Achieved Star here and fill in the form

Achieved

THROWING SHAPES

A well-aimed object can be used to distract or disarm an enemy. Photocopy and enlarge the target below and attach it to objects of different sizes and shapes (preferably unbreakable!). Place these around your backyard or local park at various heights and distances from your shooting spot and, using beanbags or tennis balls as missiles, try to knock them over.

STANDING TARGET

What objects did you
use as targets?

How far away was
your farthest target?

| 0 , 0 | feet

Did you hit it? | y/n |

Did you hit
them all? | y/n |

How many did you
knock over the first time?

| 0 , 0 | out of | 0 , 0 |

10   20   30   40   50   40   30   20   10

MOVING TARGET

Ask your sidekick to
hurl the objects into
the air. Try to hit them
before they land.

How many targets did
you hit in the air?

| 0 , 0 | out of | 0 , 0 |

Get your sidekick to
put on a helmet and a
padded jacket and to
attach a target to their
back. Then tell them
to run away from you
while you take aim . . .

How many direct hits
did you manage?

| 0 , 0 | out of | 0 , 0 |

What was the farthest
direct hit you managed?

| 0 , 0 | feet

DISARM OF THE LAW

Ask your sidekick to stand holding a dummy weapon. Make sure they're facing away from you and wearing protective clothing, like a helmet and a padded jacket and gloves. Standing some distance behind them and slightly to the side, try to knock the weapon out of their hand with your beanbag or tennis ball. If you succeed, try again, but this time as you are running past them.

Did you succeed in disarming them
from a standing position? | y/n |

If yes, how many attempts did it
take? | 0 , 0 |

Did you succeed in disarming them
as you ran past? | y/n |

If yes, how many attempts did it
take? | 0 , 0 |

If no, in either case did you decide to disarm
them with . . .   . . . your
hands? | | . . . your
feet? | | . . . your
mind? | |

At the same time you could master these other **Ways**:
10: Stealth • **25:** Control Your Temper • **33:** Anticipate Your Enemy's Next Move
49: Hone Your Moral Compass • **83:** Hand–Eye Skill • **90:** Healing

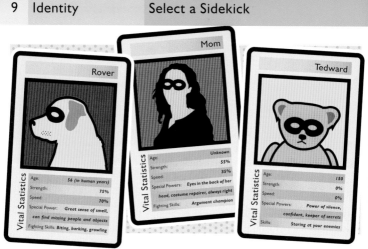

Select a Sidekick

No man's an island, and even superheroes need friends. While you're doing all the important jobs, who's going to watch your back, carry your equipment, and rub your feet at the end of a hard day's world-saving? Of course your sidekick shouldn't just be your drudge, but you do need to watch they don't get too big for their britches. Whoever you choose has to be up to the task but should also know who's the boss!

Dynamic Duos

- Who's your best friend? Whom can you trust with your life and depend on not to disappear in a cloud of dust as soon as things get a little hairy? Make a list of possible candidates and then devise a test for them to find the right person for the job.
- For your test, you might want to pick ten challenges from this book that best represent the qualities needed in your sidekick.
- Be honest and analyze where your own weaknesses lie. A sidekick could usefully plug any gaps in your skill set. For example, if you're a whiz kid but a bit of a weakling, pick someone with muscle and fitness. On the other hand, if you're the physical type but no good at the books, go for someone who's got brains. If you want to be an evil genius, you need a bodyguard more than a sidekick.
- Don't pick anyone too cool or beautiful, with amazing fashion sense or shelves lined with trophies and awards for being fabulous—they will present a threat to your own image.

> **A friend in need . . .** It's not easy to keep your identity from the world. Imagine the relief when you find someone with whom you can share your dark secrets and fears. Don't let on to the candidates what exactly they're applying for, or otherwise your cover will be blown!

Select a Sidekick Form

Once you have mastered this **Way to Become a Superhero**,
stick your Achieved Star here and fill in the form

Achieved

Sidekick Assessment

Give your applicant three different challenges from the book and see how they perform before you decide to induct them as your sidekick . . .

Applicant's name

Your relationship to applicant

Way to Become a Superhero Number . . .

| 0 | 0 | 0 | Rate their performance in this challenge | 10 |

Way to Become a Superhero Number . . .

| 0 | 0 | 0 | Rate their performance in this challenge | 10 |

Way to Become a Superhero Number . . .

| 0 | 0 | 0 | Rate their performance in this challenge | 10 |

How long have you known this person?

| 0 | 0 | Years | 0 | 0 | Months

Can you trust the applicant . . .

. . . to keep secrets?
. . . not to give up?
. . . with mental tasks?
. . . with physical tasks?
. . . with your life?

| y/n | y/n | y/n | y/n | y/n |

In conclusion, do you think they will make a good sidekick? | y/n |

If yes, give your sidekick a superhero name

Are they better than you at certain things? | y/n |

If yes, list those skills below

Ask your new sidekick to sign the confidentiality agreement below.

By signing this document I agree not to reveal your secret identity or break your trust in any way on pain of death.

Signature

Did you use this power for . . .

GOOD? or

☐ EVIL?

Applicant's most irritating characteristic

Applicant's most attractive characteristic

Place your sidekick's thumbprint above

At the same time you could master these other **Ways:**
36: Be in Two Places at Once • **37**: Train Your Superpet • **78**: Be a Good Influence
95: Build a Network of Contacts • **96**: Lead from the Front • **99**: Gather a Superteam

S.A.S. (STEALTH AND SURPRISE)

Stealth

In stealth mode you need to be focused and relaxed, so you remain steady on your feet while alert and constantly on the lookout for danger. You're allowed to breathe, but you'll only be able to do this quietly if you remain composed. Don't even try to be stealthy if you need to pee.

Art of No Noise

- Basically you need to practice creeping up on people. You might lose a friend if you do this too often on the same person, so practice on a range of victims and persuade them you're not doing it deliberately.
- Patience is vital: you can't afford to draw attention with jerky movements. Conceal yourself in a room and wait until someone comes in, then see how long you can maintain your cover.
- Ask your sidekick to stand a good distance away with their back to you, then try to sneak up and put your hands over their eyes before they detect and grab you. They only get one chance to turn and catch you, and they can't move from the spot, so you must be within reach.
- Test out shoes (thin soles are best, so you can feel the ground) and clothes to find something that gives you maximum freedom of movement and minimum noise. It's hard to be stealthy in stilettos.
- Set up a portable recording device and move stealthily around the room before creeping up on it. Listen back to see how much noise you made. Try this in various places, indoors and out, with different types of surfaces to walk across and low levels of background noise.

Stink bomb: Noise isn't the only thing that might give you away: smells can too. So make sure you're clean but neutral-smelling. That means no perfumed toiletry products, and no visits to burger, taco, or seafood restaurants before setting out on a mission.

Stealth Form

Once you have mastered this **Way to Become a Superhero**, stick your Achieved Star here and fill in the form

Achieved

———— YOU GIVE ME THE CREEPS ————

How many people can you creep up on this week? See if you can get right behind them before they notice you. You might even be able to stand there for a while. Record your attempts, even if you fail.

Name of victim 1	Name of victim 2	Name of victim 3

Location of stealth attack	Location of stealth attack	Location of stealth attack

Date m m d d y y   Date m m d d y y   Date m m d d y y

Were you detected before y/n you reached them?

Were you detected before y/n you reached them?

Were you detected before y/n you reached them?

If no, how long were you able to stand behind them before they noticed you?

If no, how long were you able to stand behind them before they noticed you?

If no, how long were you able to stand behind them before they noticed you?

0 0 : 0 0 : 0 0   0 0 : 0 0 : 0 0   0 0 : 0 0 : 0 0

When the victim spotted you, did they . . .

When the victim spotted you, did they . . .

When the victim spotted you, did they . . .

. . . flinch? y/n   . . . shriek/ gasp? y/n

. . . flinch? y/n   . . . shriek/ gasp? y/n

. . . flinch? y/n   . . . shriek/ gasp? y/n

. . . act unsurprised? y/n

. . . act unsurprised? y/n

. . . act unsurprised? y/n

. . . nearly have a heart attack? y/n

. . . nearly have a heart attack? y/n

. . . nearly have a heart attack? y/n

Are you still friends? y/n

Are you still friends? y/n

Are you still friends? y/n

Find somewhere to conceal yourself in a room and wait until someone comes in. How long can you remain hidden?

Did you use this power for . . .

Room   Hiding place

GOOD? or

Time concealed 0 0 : 0 0 : 0 0   Were you detected? y/n

EVIL?

If no, did you jump out at them or stay hidden and spy?   Surprised them   Spied on them

At the same time you could master these other **Ways**:
16: Sixth Sense • **27**: See in the Dark • **28**: Balance • **43**: Invisibility • **47**: Master of Illusion • **62**: Superhearing • **66**: Agility • **69**: Kung-Fu Master • **85**: Shape-Shift

Groom Your Dark Side

Becoming a supervillain isn't just about doing evil, it's about being evil—evil from the inside out, front to back, and upside down. It's a state of mind, a way of behaving, and a lifestyle to boot. Here are some areas to work on:

My Bad

- **Evil Laugh:** You will need this a lot. Will you go for a tittering snigger, a hysterical giggle, a cackle, a shriek, a booming guffaw, or the classic "Muahaha!"? Once you've decided, practice daily and play with it to find out how you can adapt it to different situations: from the first inkling of your evil master plan, to the moment of triumph as you realize your ambition, to the years of seclusion in the asylum.
- **Nervous Habit:** It may be finger drumming, leg jiggling, mustache twirling, or a twitching eye. Pick something to suit your style but that can act as a useful distraction and a memorable feature. Beard stroking is good too. If you don't have one yet, practice on someone else's.
- **Moody Temperament:** Supervillains find power intoxicating and don't cope well when things don't go exactly as they want. Keep henchmen and victims on edge with your unpredictable reactions—sometimes dramatic, sometimes casual, but always deliciously wicked.
- **Twisted Sense of Humor:** Hidden camera shows, horror movies, slapstick comedy, reality TV, soap operas—this is exactly the sort of entertainment you should be dining on. Make sure you have a hearty, evil laugh out loud at everyone else's expense.

 Gangstas' pastime paradise: Here are some other things villains should learn to love: spicy food, thunderstorms, practical jokes, misfits, surprises, money, shoot-'em-up video games, opera, Gothic novels, explosions, darkness, mirrors, etc. And to not love: people.

Groom Your Dark Side **Form**

Once you have mastered this **Way to Become an Evil Genius**, stick your Achieved Star here and fill in the form

Achieved

—— EVIL LAUGH ——

What is your preferred evil laugh?

A tittering snigger ☐   A hysterical giggle ☐

A cackle ☐   A high-pitched shriek ☐

A booming guffaw ☐   A loud "Muahaha!" ☐

How evil is your laugh? Ask someone to rate it out of ten [out of 10]

What did you last laugh evilly about?

—— NERVOUS HABIT ——

What is your preferred nervous habit?

A facial tic ☐   Drumming fingers ☐

Jiggling legs ☐   Nail-biting ☐

Chin/beard stroking ☐   Mustache twirling ☐

How unnerving do people find your habit? Ask someone to rate it out of ten [out of 10]

What brought on your last attack?

—— MOOD SWINGS ——

Track your mood swings over the course of an hour and record the full range of emotions below. Aim for a swing every ten minutes.

—— TWISTED HUMOR ——

Plan your week's menu of dark entertainment. It could include computer games, films, music— anything to broaden and satisfy your twisted sense of humor.

TIME	MOOD
00:00	
00:10	
00:20	
00:30	
00:40	
00:50	
01:00	

DAY	ACTIVITY
Mon	
Tue	
Wed	
Thu	
Fri	
Sat	
Sun	

At the same time you could master these other **Ways**:
1: Discover Your Alter Ego • **32**: Get a Villainous Chair • **46**: Choose a Cause
53: Be Ruthless • **56**: Invent Some Great One-Liners • **68**: Survive Your Fatal Flaw

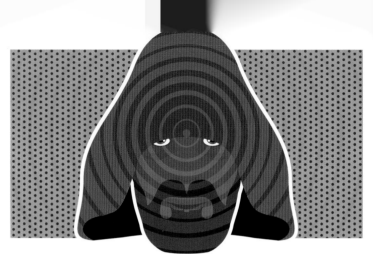

Mind Control

Breaking in and controlling someone else's mind is akin to hacking into the Pentagon's computers: it's hard, but it has been done before. From getting someone to obey your commands (aka the "Jedi mind trick") to stealing or erasing memories, mind control is one of the greatest weapons of all.

Don't Mind Me

- It's possible to influence someone's behavior by subtly echoing their movements. Make sure you're in their sight line, but don't be obvious as you copy what they do. Gradually you should be able to take control. Try scratching your nose or yawning and see if your subject follows suit.
- Learn the art of hypnosis, and start by practicing on yourself. This will enable you to bolster your mind's defenses against attempts to control it by your enemies. You need to be deeply relaxed, so find somewhere you won't be interrupted and practice emptying your mind of all thoughts. Then focus on one image—a corridor or staircase—and slowly travel down it. Feel yourself becoming more weightless with every step. Once you're in a hypnotic trance, you can feed your mind positive suggestions like, "Your mind is your own. You have complete control over it."
- Next you need to master conversational hypnosis, so you can control someone's mind without them even knowing it. You must first establish a good rapport with your victim to relax them, then find ways to drop coded suggestions into conversation (perhaps in the form of anecdotes) that their subconscious can process and absorb as instructions. Try it.

Brainwashing: There are cruder methods of mind control that are likely to appeal more to supervillains. They include threats, intimidation, propaganda, kidnapping—any kind of nasty psychological pressure. But, of course, we don't recommend those.

Mind Control Form

Once you have mastered this **Way to Become a Superhero**, stick your Achieved Star here and fill in the form

Achieved

———— DO AS I DO ————

Go to a cafe and take a seat where you're in another customer's line of sight. Start echoing their movements, but be subtle about it—you don't want them to know that you're watching them. After a few minutes, take control and begin to lead the actions. See if they copy you.

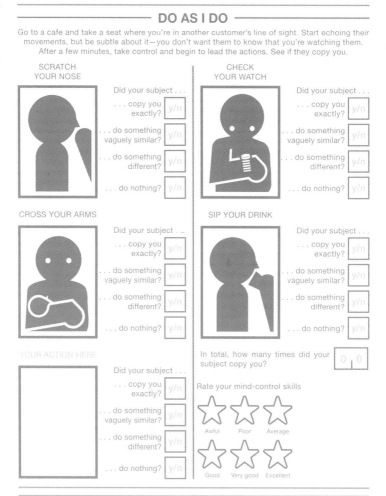

SCRATCH YOUR NOSE

Did your subject . . .

. . . copy you exactly? [y/n]

. . . do something vaguely similar? [y/n]

. . . do something different? [y/n]

. . . do nothing? [y/n]

CHECK YOUR WATCH

Did your subject . . .

. . . copy you exactly? [y/n]

. . . do something vaguely similar? [y/n]

. . . do something different? [y/n]

. . . do nothing? [y/n]

CROSS YOUR ARMS

Did your subject . . .

. . . copy you exactly? [y/n]

. . . do something vaguely similar? [y/n]

. . . do something different? [y/n]

. . . do nothing? [y/n]

SIP YOUR DRINK

Did your subject . . .

. . . copy you exactly? [y/n]

. . . do something vaguely similar? [y/n]

. . . do something different? [y/n]

. . . do nothing? [y/n]

YOUR ACTION HERE

Did your subject . . .

. . . copy you exactly? [y/n]

. . . do something vaguely similar? [y/n]

. . . do something different? [y/n]

. . . do nothing? [y/n]

In total, how many times did your subject copy you? [0 | 0]

Rate your mind-control skills

☆ Awful   ☆ Poor   ☆ Average

☆ Good   ☆ Very good   ☆ Excellent

At the same time you could master these other **Ways**:
7: Decipher Devious Riddles • **40**: Understand Body Language • **78**: Be a Good Influence
92: Telepathy • **93**: Develop Powers of Persuasion • **101**: Save the World from Yourself

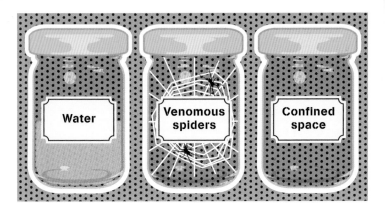

Conquer Your Fears

It's okay to be afraid. Unless you're incapable of love (i.e., mega evil) or immortal and able to bring the dead back to life, you'll fear for your own safety or others' at times, even when that fear is irrational. What's vital is that you don't let fear stop you from doing the right thing or taking risks.

The Best Defense Is a Good Offense

- List the five things you dread the most. Are they physical things (e.g., a type of creature or a person), conditions (e.g., being high up or enclosed), or something more abstract (e.g., rejection or death)? Describe what it is about each thing that frightens you. The more you understand where fear comes from, the better placed you are to confront it. Are any fears related to bad past experiences, for example?
- Which fears are irrational and which are justifiable because the thing you fear can really hurt you? How much can they hurt you? How likely are you to be faced with them? If they're potentially fatal and the risks are high, you're right to fear them, and until you've mastered all the other superpowers, you're not in a position to confront them head-on.
- When facing your fears, set yourself a time limit, then increase the length of exposure by gradual degrees until you have fully conquered your fear. You could also ask a family member or friend to accompany you the first time, until you feel confident to face your fear alone.
- Complete the test on the opposite page and see how you fare when you have to face up to the most common fears.

Grin and bear it: Don't underestimate the power of positive thinking—it will help you to banish those negative thoughts as you confront the thing you fear most. So bring to mind your happiest memories, or do as Peter Pan advised and think happy thoughts.

Conquer Your Fears **Form**

Once you have mastered this **Way to Become a Superhero**, stick your Achieved Star here and fill in the form

★ **Achieved**

CONFRONT YOUR FEARS

Below you'll find some of the most common phobias, and space for you to enter one of your own personal phobias. Your challenge is to confront these fears and overcome them.

SPIDERS
Hold a spider!

Risk factor | 10 |

How big was the spider?

How long did you hold it for?

| 0 , 0 | mins | 0 , 0 | secs

How hard was it to do?

Easy | Okay | Hard | Impossible

Have you conquered your fear? | y/n |

SMALL PLACES
Sit down in a closet

Risk factor | 10 |

How small was the closet?

How long did you stay in it for?

| 0 , 0 | mins | 0 , 0 | secs

How hard was it to do?

Easy | Okay | Hard | Impossible

Have you conquered your fear? | y/n |

HEIGHTS Go to the top floor of a skyscraper and check out the view

Risk factor | 10 |

How high was the building?

How long did you look down for?

| 0 , 0 | mins | 0 , 0 | secs

How hard was it to do?

Easy | Okay | Hard | Impossible

Have you conquered your fear? | y/n |

DEATH Take a walk around a cemetery!

Risk factor | 10 |

How many ghosts did you see?

How long was your walk?

| 0 , 0 | mins | 0 , 0 | secs

How hard was it to do?

Easy | Okay | Hard | Impossible

Have you conquered your fear? | y/n |

YOUR FEAR

Write your fear here

Write your challenge here

Why are you afraid of this?

How long did you confront your fear for? | 0 , 0 | mins | 0 , 0 | secs

Did you use this power for...

How hard was it to do?

Easy | Okay | Hard | Impossible

GOOD? or **EVIL?**

Risk factor | 10 |

Have you conquered your fear? | y/n |

At the same time you could master these other **Ways**:
44: Never Give Up • **45**: Save the World from Scary Monsters • **60**: Save the World from the Undead • **70**: Cope Under Pressure • **84**: Resist Temptation • **98**: Swim Like a Fish

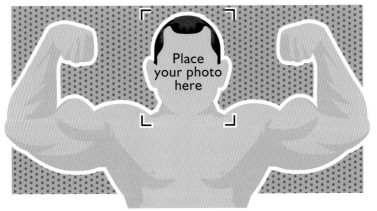

Strength

Some people think being superhuman is all about strength. They pump themselves up to develop oversized muscles and spend hours training to pull trucks and toss kegs—like that helps anyone. Remember the story of David and Goliath? You don't have to be a beefcake to be a superhero, but admittedly some above-average level of strength will come in handy.

Muscling in on the (Criminal) Act

- From now on, if there's a stubborn jar lid that needs removing in your household, you are the person for the job. Be the one to carry the heavy shopping bags, move the furniture around when required, and turn off stiff, dripping faucets. Oh, and you may wish to do some secret weight training in your bedroom too. Monitor your progress with regular arm-wrestling contests with willing family and friends.
- Ask your sidekick to clench their hands into fists—as if gripping the sides of a steering wheel—to place one fist on top of the other, and then to push their elbows together. They must use all their strength to hold this position while you place your right index finger on the back of their left fist, your left index finger on the back of their right fist, and give a gentle push in opposite directions. However hard they try to keep their fists together, you should be able to push them apart easily.
- As your powers develop, remember to think before throwing a ball or shaking someone's hand. You don't want to give yourself away. It will require a conscious effort to appear feebler than you really are.

Supertots: Some people are born with myostatin-related muscle hypertrophy, a rare condition that increases muscle mass and reduces body mass. Liam Hoekstra is one such case. At nine months old, he could do pull-ups and climb up and down stairs.

Strength Form

Once you have mastered this **Way to Become a Superhero**, stick your Achieved Star here and fill in the form

Achieved

——— STRONGMAN ———

How much weight can you lift? You don't want to injure yourself in training, so remember to place your feet shoulder-width apart and keep your back straight. Tighten your stomach muscles and lift slowly, using the muscles in your arms and legs. Complete the poster below when you've discovered the limits of your strength . . .

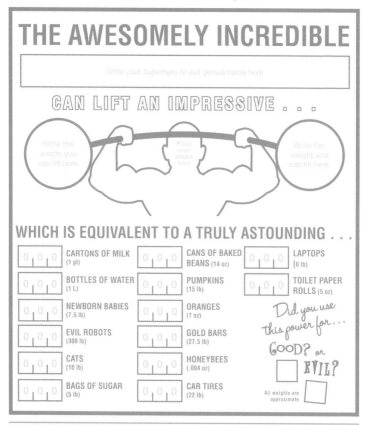

THE AWESOMELY INCREDIBLE

Write your superhero or evil genius name here

CAN LIFT AN IMPRESSIVE . . .

Write the weight you can lift here

Place your photo here

Write the weight you can lift here

WHICH IS EQUIVALENT TO A TRULY ASTOUNDING . . .

0 0 0 CARTONS OF MILK (1 pt)	0 0 0 CANS OF BAKED BEANS (14 oz)	0 0 0 LAPTOPS (6 lb)
0 0 0 BOTTLES OF WATER (1 L)	0 0 0 PUMPKINS (15 lb)	0 0 0 TOILET PAPER ROLLS (5 oz)
0 0 0 NEWBORN BABIES (7.5 lb)	0 0 0 ORANGES (7 oz)	Did you use this power for . . .
0 0 0 EVIL ROBOTS (300 lb)	0 0 0 GOLD BARS (27.5 lb)	GOOD? or
0 0 0 CATS (10 lb)	0 0 0 HONEYBEES (.004 oz)	☐ EVIL?
0 0 0 BAGS OF SUGAR (5 lb)	0 0 0 CAR TIRES (22 lb)	☐ All weights are approximate

At the same time you could master these other **Ways**:
6: Stamina • **28**: Balance • **39**: Speed • **69**: Kung-Fu Master • **98**: Swim Like a Fish

Save the World from Rampaging Robots

Anyone who works or plays on computers will know only too well that these man-made machines can be rebellious, obstinate, and deep-down evil. So far this may have meant losing that long essay you spent hours writing or failing to complete the last level in a game because your computer crashes just at the vital moment. But what about when our technology turns against us on a *Terminator* scale?

Microchip on Your Shoulder

- If you have the technical expertise, you could build robots bigger and better than your enemy. But this will take time you may not have. The other method is to design a computer virus you can download into the robot's system (or mainframe computer controlling the robot army).
- If attacked by a robot that can change into any shape and self-repair, you should attack while it's in mid-transformation. Disperse the blobs and keep them apart at all costs before you incinerate them so that they merge with less evil metals.
- If attacked by giant walking robots, your best bet is to go for the legs. Make them trip or slip or lure them into a pit—then take 'em out.
- Robots may be cleverer than us, they may be stronger, faster, and more deadly, but at the end of the day, they can't do a whole lot of anything if they run out of power. Find out what they run on and how they recharge, then do what you can to prevent them from getting to their power supply. If they're solar-powered, you could be in trouble.

> **We come in pieces:** Don't bother trying to negotiate with evil robots. They aren't like WALL-E. They don't possess any human feelings or sympathies to which you can appeal. They'll lie, cheat, and kill without blinking an eyelid (a lack of eyelids helps).

Save the World . . .
from Rampaging Robots Form

Once you have mastered this **Way to Become a Superhero**,
stick your Achieved Star here and fill in the form

Achieved

RAMPAGING ROBOTS
——— KNOW YOUR ENEMY ———

Spot the early warning signs of a robot rebellion and take appropriate measures.

Have any of your household appliances been behaving suspiciously? [y/n]

If yes, which one(s)?

Robot weaknesses

What are they doing?

Robot strengths

Turning on or off by themselves [ ]

Sparking/ melting [ ]

Making angry beeping noises [ ]

Having a major malfunction [ ]

Ignoring your instructions [ ]

Trying to kill you [ ]

Have you also observed any of the following?

Out-of- control cars [y/n]

Sadistic elevators/ automatic doors [y/n]

Internet/radio/ TV interference [y/n]

Malfunctioning traffic signals [y/n]

YOU NEED A PLAN OF ACTION. WILL YOU . . .	Explain how you will carry out your plan below
. . . install better anti-virus software? [y/n]	
. . . shut down all power sources? [y/n]	
. . . try to reason with the computers? [y/n]	
. . . design your own computer virus? [y/n]	
. . . try to hack into the computer systems and take control? [y/n]	

Place a photo of your rebellious technology here

Did you use this power for . . .
GOOD? or [ ]
EVIL? [ ]

At the same time you could master these other **Ways**:
33: Anticipate Your Enemy's Next Move • **41**: Become a Science Genius
73: Create a Force Field • **79**: Design Your Own Gadgets • **94**: Talk to Computers

Sixth Sense

Being at the top of the food chain for so long has meant we've lost touch with our sixth sense. We've become complacent and disregard instinct as irrational. But if you've ever said something like, "I've got a bad feeling about this," there's a chance you can reengage with your survival instincts.

Danger Ranger

- Wherever you go, always plan out the escape routes and what objects may be used for attack or defense if need be. Relax your mind, shutting off all distractions, and allow your senses to reach hyperawareness so you can pick up on unusual signs in your surroundings, however small, such as shadows, reflections, gusts of air or sudden stillness, or scents and sounds carried in the wind. Be aware of how you feel and let this be your radar to danger before conscious thought takes over.
- Fear can be our friend as well as our enemy, alerting us to danger. For a week, carry this book (or a notebook) with you and make a record of each time you sense your brain's warning signals, for example when you're crossing the road, saying good-bye to someone you love, or hearing a strange noise. Rate these uneasy feelings for intensity and describe the physical sensations that accompany them.
- Animals are believed to have a greater alertness to danger because, in addition to other acute senses, they can detect subtle vibrations in the ground. Clothing and footwear mean the fine hairs covering our bodies are desensitized, so get au naturel and try to tune in to your hairy sensors.

 You make me sick: Some creatures employ interesting warning signals that act effectively as defense too. For example, squids squirt ink when they sense danger, and some birds, like vultures, vomit on anything they feel threatened by. Are there lessons to be learned here?

Sixth Sense **Form**

Once you have mastered this **Way to Become a Superhero**, stick your Achieved Star here and fill in the form

Achieved

--- **SENSATIONAL DANGER** ---

Using the form below, keep a record of the times your sixth sense seems to be alerting you to danger.

Date | Time | Location | Danger sense intensity | 5

m m d d y y y y | : |

What were you doing? | How did you feel?

External signs of danger (if any):

Date | Time | Location | Danger sense intensity | 5

m m d d y y y y | : |

What were you doing? | How did you feel?

External signs of danger (if any):

Date | Time | Location | Danger sense intensity | 5

m m d d y y y y | : |

What were you doing? | How did you feel?

External signs of danger (if any):

In any of the cases above, did your sixth sense help you to identify a real threat? | y/n

What form did that threat take?

If yes, who was in danger?

What action did you take to neutralize the threat?

* If you answered "no," that doesn't necessarily mean you have a faulty sixth sense. Keep monitoring it—one day it could save someone's life!

Did you use this power for...
GOOD? *or*
☐ **EVIL?**
☐

At the same time you could master these other **Ways**:
5: Super-Vision • **33**: Anticipate Your Enemy's Next Move • **34**: Supersmell • **50**: Second Sight • **60**: Save the World from the Undead • **62**: Superhearing • **63**: Observation Skills

Choose Your Outfit

A pair of underpants worn on the outside might work for some, but this isn't about making bold fashion statements (or blunders). The need to combine a sensational look with function and comfort has never been greater. Fashion is here today, gone tomorrow, but a superhero is here to stay.

Dressed to Kill

- Make a list of the practical requirements of your outfit. For example, do you need a tool belt or any built-in mechanisms on, say, your wrists or ankles? Every outfit should be waterproof, but if you're especially amphibious, you might need some breathing apparatus. Or how about built-in wings to stay airborne? It's all very well to have an eye-catching look, but what if the key to your success is stealth?

- Your outfit should send a clear message about who you are and what you do. It is part of brand You, so color and style are important and should tie in with the other elements that make you a powerful icon. And if you haven't done so already, you should really design a logo for yourself that you can incorporate onto your clothing.

- How are you going to disguise your identity? Will it be with some sort of headgear or makeup—or a mixture of the two?

- Once your design is there, experiment with prototypes until you have perfected it. Be creative in the fabrics and materials you use. Practice putting your outfit on and taking it off quickly, and test it for comfort, durability, and special features in the privacy of your own secret base.

Tops and tights: Capes, masks, tights, body armor, gloves, boots, and plenty of tight-fitting spandex are firm favorites in the superhero's wardrobe. Consider why and if you need them too. Beware the giveaway mask-print on your face when you change out of your outfit.

Choose Your Outfit **Form**

Once you have mastered this **Way to Become a Superhero**,
stick your Achieved Star here and fill in the form

Achieved

WEAR IT OUT

Name your three main colors

Name your top three practical considerations

Costumed

Draw your outfit design here

Does your outfit help you to . . .

. . . fly? [y/n] If yes, how?

Your answer here

. . . swim? [y/n] If yes, how?

Your answer here

. . . climb? [y/n] If yes, how?

Your answer here

. . . be stealthy? [y/n] If yes, how?

Your answer here

. . . defend yourself? [y/n] If yes, how?

Your answer here

Place a photo of you in your finished outfit here

Did you incorporate any special features? If yes, list them in the box below

Did you use this power for... GOOD? or [ ] EVIL? [ ]

Grade your outfit out of 5 for the following:

Comfort [5] Looks [5] Ability to disguise you [5] Practicality [5]

At the same time you could master these other **Ways**:
1: Discover Your Alter Ego • **2**: Choose Your Name • **24**: Design a Logo
42: Strike a Superhero Pose • **43**: Invisibility • **79**: Design Your Own Gadgets

Harness the Elements

The force of nature is superior to that of any single human being, so it's no surprise that superheroes and supervillains have made various attempts to harness some of that power and use it for their own ends.

Earth, Wind, and Fire (and Water)

- Harness the power of water by gathering it in a balloon and hurling it at your enemies. A well-aimed water pistol can also wreak havoc.
- Harness the power of fire by making your own wax candles. That way, you're set if the lights ever go out! You can start with single-color candles, and work your way up to beautiful multicolor candles.
- Harness the power of wind using an old, clean mini-yogurt container and a balloon. Tie a knot in the neck of the balloon, without first blowing it up, then snip the other end off (the wider top end). Stretch the open end of the balloon over the top of the yogurt container. Lastly, cut a small hole in the base of the container. If you pull back on the knot of the balloon and release it, you should be able to send an air bolt out of the hole. That's the basic concept. You can design your own bigger, better version.
- Harness the power of the earth by making the most of what it offers you. For example, a bit of water and earth creates mud—great for camouflage and flinging at your enemies. Use trees as vantage points, navigational aids, and hideouts. Get creative and write a manual of the ways your environment can offer means of defense and offense.

 Red in tooth and claw: So you're not summoning volcanoes, floods, quakes, or storms, but that's no bad thing. Such elemental beasts act indiscriminately on anyone unlucky enough to be in their path. Messing with them is a dangerous business and risks high casualty numbers.

Harness the Elements Form

Once you have mastered this **Way to Become a Superhero**, stick your Achieved Star here and fill in the form

Achieved

FIRE

Harness the power of fire by making your own wax candle (and make sure you harness some water or wind too, in case you want to put out your candle).

WHAT YOU NEED: primed wicks, scissors, wax, dye (for color), double boiler, a jam jar (or other container)

1. Get your wick ready. Cut it so that it is approximately 1 inch longer than the full height of your candle. Don't put the wick in the jam jar just yet.
2. Melt the wax and dye together inside the double boiler. Make sure a parent is there to help you with the stove!
3. Carefully pour the melted wax into the jam jar. As the wax begins to harden, insert the wick into the middle of the jar.
4. Let it cool.

How long did it take you to create your candle?

5–10 mins ☐	10–20 mins ☐
20–30 mins ☐	I gave up ☐

WIND

Harness the power of the wind by making an air blaster. You'll find instructions on the opposite page.

Balloon

Hole

Yogurt container

Fire your air blaster at a piece of paper scrunched up into a ball. Keep moving the paper ball back to test the range of your air blaster.

Did your air blaster work? ☐ y/n

What was the top range of your blaster? ☐0,0 . ☐0,0 in

What/who else did you fire your blaster at?

EARTH

Harness the power of Mother Nature by finding ingenious ways to utilize your surroundings.

Have you ever used Mother Nature to provide camouflage? ☐ y/n

If yes, how?

Have you ever used Mother Nature to provide cover? ☐ y/n

If yes, how?

Have you ever used Mother Nature to provide food? ☐ y/n

If yes, how?

Have you ever used Mother Nature to provide shelter? ☐ y/n

If yes, how?

WATER

Harness the power of water . . . in several balloons. Bombs away!

Who was your target?

A tree ☐	Your nemesis ☐	Your sidekick ☐

Other (please specify)

How many bombs hit their target? ☐0,0

Did you use this power for . . .

GOOD? or

EVIL?

Did your target return fire? ☐ y/n

How many times were you hit? ☐0,0

At the same time you could master these other **Ways**:
41: Become a Science Genius • **58**: Withstand Heat and Cold • **75**: Save the World from Environmental Disaster • **79**: Design Your Own Gadgets • **98**: Swim Like a Fish

Know Whom to Save First

You can't save everybody. You're not some kind of god, you're just an ordinary person with extraordinary powers. But until scientists come up with a way to clone people, it's still just you against the world. This means it's vital that you know your priorities.

Do the Math

- Women and children first—that's the standard advice. However, there are other considerations. In an end-of-the-world scenario where you can only save a handful of people, shouldn't they include those best qualified to rebuild human civilization? It might be great to have the world's best baseball player to throw a ball around with when the world's gone to ruin, but it would be more useful to have someone with practical skills, like an engineer, a carpenter, or a doctor. A mix of male and female would be helpful too, for obvious reasons.

- Make a list of the worst crimes and most pressing disasters. Helping a kid whose homework was about to fall out of his bag into a puddle would probably come lower down on your list of priorities than saving the human race, whose very existence was threatened by an army of despotic robots. But other choices will be harder to make.

- Your first instinct may be to save your family and friends, or the boy or girl you like*—but sometimes you have to trust they can look after themselves while you attend to the masses. When it comes to saving human lives, it's got to be quantity over quality.

---

 *If you love someone let them go: Imagine if you went to the trouble of saving the boy or girl of your dreams, only for them to go off with someone else. That would leave a bitter taste in your mouth and make you forever wish you'd saved your pet hamster instead.

Know Whom to Save First **Form**

Once you have mastered this **Way to Become a Superhero**,
stick your Achieved Star here and fill in the form

Achieved

——— SAVE ME, SAVE ME!!! ———

Fill in the pyramid chart to show who you would save in order of priority. Write their names or
professions in the spaces provided. You'll find some ideas down the sides of the page.

PROFESSIONALS

Doctor
Politician
Lawyer
Scientist
TV personality
Pop star
Mail carrier
Construction worker
Pharmacist
Engineer
Astronaut
Police officer
Nuclear physicist
Secret agent
Baseball player
Carpenter
Athlete
Writer
Zoologist
Chemist
Nurse
Comedian
Surgeon
Chef

PEOPLE YOU KNOW

Mom
Dad
Sister
Brother
Girfriend
Boyfriend
Ex-girfriend
Ex-boyfriend
Grandma
Grandpa
Nemesis
Pet
Best friend
Teacher
Classmates
Neighbors
Uncles
Aunts
Cousins

Place
your photo
here

At the same time you could master these other **Ways**:
20: Learn to Multitask • **29**: Solve Impossible Problems • **54**: Make Sacrifices
81: Make the Right Decisions—Fast • **99**: Gather a Superteam

Learn to Multitask

Time is not a luxury you will be lucky enough to have in most emergencies, so being able to do several things at once is a vital skill to learn. Still, there'll always be a limit to how much you can take on.

Task Master

- Combining a mental activity with a physical one is the easiest way to multitask. Most people can manage to run or exercise while listening to music or chatting, but throwing a ball up in the air and catching it while reciting the 13 times table will definitely require more skill—or juggling while answering rapid-fire questions about quantum physics. Devise a training plan with your sidekick that gradually builds up the difficulty of the simultaneous activities.
- Doing two physical tasks at the same time might be impossible—as a superhero, you're not suddenly going to grow extra limbs (well, it's unlikely). But you can train your feet to carry out tasks normally done by hand, like picking things up or typing, and learn to do things faster than the average human, so that you can get more accomplished.
- The brain cannot consciously do more than one mental task at a time: the skill is in switching rapidly between tasks and identifying which takes priority. Do the "Double Trouble" challenge on the opposite page. Is it quicker to solve all the number problems first, then the word ones, or to keep swapping between them? Time yourself. For your next challenge, set yourself a listening test at the same time as a visual one.

> **Autopilot:** You may not be able to consciously do two tasks at the same time, but what things can you do well without focusing on them? Try doing something you think you're good at while watching TV. Did your usual high standards on that other activity slip?

Learn to Multitask **Form**

Once you have mastered this **Way to Become a Superhero**, stick your Achieved Star here and fill in the form

☆ Achieved

SIGN ON

The only real way to multitask is to get all your hands and feet working for you. How ambidextrous are you?

With your dominant hand, write your full name below

[ ]

Which is your dominant hand?

Left [ ]   Right [ ]

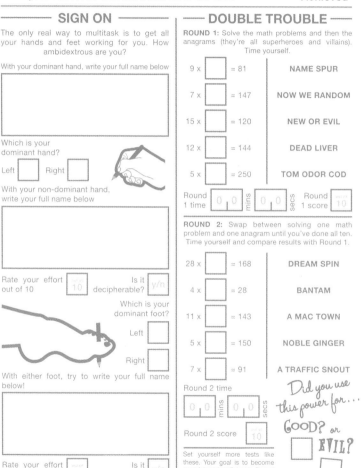

With your non-dominant hand, write your full name below

[ ]

Rate your effort out of 10 [/10]   Is it decipherable? [y/n]

Which is your dominant foot?

Left [ ]

Right [ ]

With either foot, try to write your full name below!

[ ]

Rate your effort out of 10 [/10]   Is it decipherable? [y/n]

DOUBLE TROUBLE

ROUND 1: Solve the math problems and then the anagrams (they're all superheroes and villains). Time yourself.

9 x [ ] = 81   **NAME SPUR**

7 x [ ] = 147   **NOW WE RANDOM**

15 x [ ] = 120   **NEW OR EVIL**

12 x [ ] = 144   **DEAD LIVER**

5 x [ ] = 250   **TOM ODOR COD**

Round 1 time [0 , 0] mins [0 , 0] secs   Round 1 score [/10]

ROUND 2: Swap between solving one math problem and one anagram until you've done all ten. Time yourself and compare results with Round 1.

28 x [ ] = 168   **DREAM SPIN**

4 x [ ] = 28   **BANTAM**

11 x [ ] = 143   **A MAC TOWN**

5 x [ ] = 150   **NOBLE GINGER**

7 x [ ] = 91   **A TRAFFIC SNOUT**

Round 2 time [0 , 0] mins [0 , 0] secs

Round 2 score [/10]

Set yourself more tests like these. Your goal is to become as quick and proficient in Round 2 as you are in Round 1.

Did you use this power for... GOOD? *or* [ ] EVIL? [ ]

At the same time you could master these other **Ways**:
1: Discover Your Alter Ego • **14**: Strength • **21**: Dexterity • **29**: Solve Impossible Problems • **36**: Be in Two Places at Once • **59**: Take Risks • **70**: Cope Under Pressure

Dexterity

Superheroes have to be able to move fast—and not just on their feet. From defusing bombs to hacking into computer systems or hand-to-hand combat with your nemesis, it's unlikely you'll find yourself with a leisurely afternoon to face these challenges one at a time. And if you're having to do two things at once, it'll be very handy to be handy with both hands, so no lax lefts or reluctant rights: ambidextrous is the aim.

Knowledge at Your Fingertips

- If you have a sidekick to deal with fan mail and complaints, it's quite possible you don't get much practice on a keyboard, but being able to touch-type is a sure sign of manual dexterity, so set yourself some tests and mark them for speed and accuracy.
- It might be hard to picture your superhero self with a pair of knitting needles (unless you're Super-Gram), but knitting is an excellent way to combat clumsiness. Okay, if you can't face that, then how about cards? See if you can master some of the more flamboyant shuffling techniques and deal faster than a dealer in a casino.
- Draw the most complicated thing you can think of—like a skeleton or a bowl of spaghetti or the engine of a car. Easy? Right, now cut it out.
- So you think you've mastered these arts? Now switch hands. See if you can spend an hour being right-handed if you're left, and left-handed if you're right. Increase the amount of time until you get through an entire day doing all the things you would normally do.

Go finger: We can all make different signs with our hands, like a thumbs-up or victory sign, but have you ever made up your own? Put together a complex routine of hand movements and performed it to music? Start a new craze. Call it finger-disco.

Dexterity Form

Once you have mastered this **Way to Become a Superhero**, stick your Achieved Star here and fill in the form

Achieved

DYPING & DEXTING

Test your dexterity with the challenges below. If your dexterity skills are poor the first time, try again—after all, practice makes perfect. Soon your fingers will be flying at the speed of light—but will your brain be able to keep up?

TYPING TEST

Type out the paragraph below as fast and as accurately as you can. Ask your sidekick to time you and check for mistakes afterward.

I was in the middle of releasing Her Majesty from the evil knots (I think they must have been double) binding her to her throne, while, with the other hand, reprogramming Doctor Dismal's rocket launcher with the coordinates of his own base (Lat: 46N 25' 4.49" and Long: 81W 17' 26.1"), when I heard a faint clattering noise. It sounded like a million knitting needles cascading down the corridors of the palace. I turned in time to see a pool of shiny black beetle-shaped nanorobots spilling under the door and heading toward us fast, each with a pair of tiny red flashing LEDs for eyes.

How fast did you type the paragraph? `0 0 0 0` secs

How many mistakes did you make? `0 0`

Dexterity rating `10`

For more tests, try here: **www.typingtest.com**

TEXT TEST

How fast can you text? Pedro Matias from Portugal broke the Guinness World Record for speed texting on January 14, 2010, when he texted the phrase below during the LG Mobile Worldcup World Championship. It took him 119 seconds. Can you beat him?

The telephone was invented by Alexander Graham Bell (UK), who filed his patent for the telephone on 14 February 1876 at the New York Patent Office, USA. The first intelligible call occurred in March 1876 in Boston, Massachusetts, when Bell phoned his assistant in a nearby room and said "Come here, Watson, I want you."

Dexterity rating `10`

Did you use this power for...

GOOD? or

EVIL?

How fast did you text the paragraph? `0 0 0 0` secs

How many mistakes did you make? `0 0`

At the same time you could master these other **Ways**:
20: Learn to Multitask • **66**: Agility • **83**: Hand–Eye Skill • **94**: Talk to Computers

Communicate with Animals

Animals can do things that humans can only dream of. Imagine if you could tap into this power by becoming allies with our feathered, furred, and finned companions. In order for friendships to flourish, though, you have the small matter of the communication barrier to overcome.

Pigeon Whispering

- Choose a variety of animal subjects—ones you can make regular contact with and that have skills you could put to good use. Don't just pick the obviously intelligent ones. A herd of sheep could slow down a fugitive criminal, for example, or a pigeon delivering its gift of white goo in your enemy's eyes could prevent them from carrying out some heinous act.
- Observe how your animal subjects use their bodies and voices to communicate with each other and with other species. Note how they respond to different situations and how they express happiness, anger, or fear.
- Practice imitating those sounds and any physical behavior that goes with them. Of course this won't always be possible—if a dog wags its tail, you may have a problem. So come up with your own equivalent: something your animal subjects will recognize and respond to.
- Once you've grasped the basics, see if you can get them to understand simple commands, and start building up a relationship with them. It's vital to get them on your side by offering food, protection, advice—whatever they need—so that they'll be willing to trust you and help you out when you call on them for assistance.

Smooth walking: When you first approach an animal, make yourself seem as non-threatening as you can. This might mean trying to look smaller, moving very slowly and smoothly, and making soothing noises. Don't wear bright colors or strong scents either.

Communicate with Animals **Form**

Once you have mastered this **Way to Become a Superhero**, stick your Achieved Star here and fill in the form

Achieved

───── WOOF, WOOF! ─────

Make your own animal phrase book. Complete the form below to get you started. You should add further phrases as you learn them. Make a note of the sounds your animal makes (if any), spelling them as you would say them, and also record any physical behavior used to communicate these phrases to you.

What animal language have you chosen to study?

PHRASE IN ENGLISH	IN _____ (your animal here) LANGUAGE SOUNDS LIKE	IN _____ (your animal here) LANGUAGE LOOKS LIKE
HELLO		
THANK YOU		
GO AWAY		
GIVE ME THAT		
I LOVE YOU		
I HATE YOU		
I DON'T LIKE THAT		
I LIKE THAT		
I'M HUNGRY		
YOUR PHRASE HERE		
YOUR PHRASE HERE		
YOUR PHRASE HERE		
YOUR PHRASE HERE		

Try using your newly learned animal phrases on your animal subject. How did you do?

No response, no understanding ☐

They responded well but I didn't understand their response ☐

I think they understood but chose to ignore me ☐

Great—we had a whole conversation ☐

Did you use this power for...

GOOD? ☐ or **EVIL?** ☐

At the same time you could master these other **Ways**:
37: Train Your Superpet • **40**: Understand Body Language • **72**: Speak a Hundred Languages • **85**: Shape-Shift • **88**: Acquire Specialist Knowledge • **92**: Telepathy

Plan for World Domination

World domination won't happen in an afternoon. Plans of this scale require stages. Break yours down into missions, each with clearly stated primary and secondary objectives, and set a date for achieving them.

It's a Dog-Eat-Dog World

• Life is structured around food chains and you have to work your way up. Draw a diagram and show where you think you are now and where you'd like to be (i.e., at the top). Then work out a route to get you there, picking out your targets. It could take time before you come close enough to the big cheeses to wolf 'em down.

• How will you fund your venture? Business deals, kidnap, cloning, blackmail, theft, bribery? Or perhaps a bit of general ass-kicking. Maybe you want to build up funds in a clean way to avoid suspicion and to allow you to work your evil from the inside.

• Who will help you? Do favors for people in order to store up favors owed to you. Get yourself well positioned to gather intelligence that may help you. Know your strengths and play to them.

• What will be your weapon of choice? Armies of zombies? A financial meltdown? A computer virus? An enormous space laser? Mother Nature? Mind-controlling drugs? Robots? Aliens?

• Identify any threats to your plan's success (e.g., superheroes) and work out how best to neutralize them. Know your weaknesses and plan for them. Bring in henchmen to supply the skills you don't have.

Business model: As part of your preparation, you should build a model of the scene of your final assault. Where are your targets and how are you going to approach them? Look for escape routes in case some interfering superhero decides to crash your party.

Plan for World Domination **Form**

Once you have mastered this **Way to Become an Evil Genius**, stick your Achieved Star here and fill in the form

Achieved

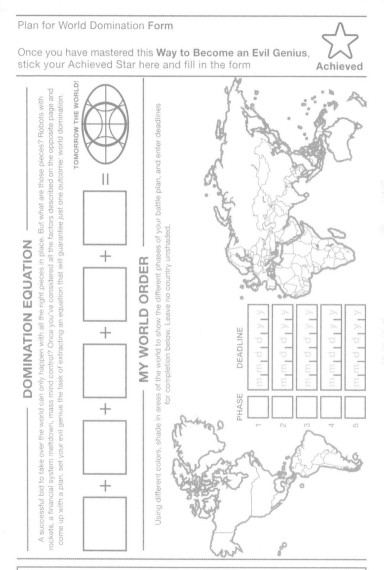

DOMINATION EQUATION

A successful bid to take over the world can only happen with all the right pieces in place. But what are those pieces? Robots with rockets, a financial system meltdown, mass mind control? Once you've considered all the factors described on the opposite page and come up with a plan, set your evil genius the task of extracting an equation that will guarantee just one outcome: world domination.

☐ + ☐ + ☐ + ☐ + ☐ =

TOMORROW THE WORLD!

MY WORLD ORDER

Using different colors, shade in areas of the world to show the different phases of your battle plan, and enter deadlines for completion below. Leave no country unshaded.

PHASE	DEADLINE
1	m m d d y y
2	m m d d y y
3	m m d d y y
4	m m d d y y
5	m m d d y y

At the same time you could master these other **Ways**:
20: Learn to Multitask • **29**: Solve Impossible Problems • **46**: Choose a Cause
53: Be Ruthless • **82**: Get a Head for Business • **97**: Know What's Happening Everywhere

Design a Logo

After you've picked a name for yourself, this really should be the next step in building brand You. You'll be able to use your logo on your costumes, stationery, vehicles, and equipment, and it might make a handy call sign.

Logo-istics

- The key to a good logo is making it easily recognizable. So when you're sketching out a few ideas, try to keep it simple and bold. This will also mean it's easier to reproduce and more versatile to use.
- Trying to encapsulate you, what you stand for, and your style in a bit of graphic design is a real challenge. You need to think outside the box, especially if your name relies on some abstract quality (like speed), rather than a physical thing (like a spider). Of course, you can use words as part of your logo, but bear in mind that an image is more universally understood than one language. If you do use words (like your name), consider what style of type is appropriate too.
- How will you reproduce your logo? If you can draw it on a computer, so much the better, as you can print it off on letterhead (if, for example, you need to send a letter to the head of police or your nemesis) or on sticky labels (so you can plaster it on all your equipment). You can even print it on special transfer paper—that means you can iron it onto your clothes or turn it into a tattoo. If you don't have a computer or the skills to reproduce it, there are other methods, such as the faithful old potato print.

 Apple, swoosh, and Golden Arches: List what you consider to be the ten most iconic logos and ask your sidekick to do the same. Are your lists quite similar? What makes these particular logos stick in the mind? Is it just that they've been around a long time?

Design a Logo **Form**

Once you have mastered this **Way to Become a Superhero**, stick your Achieved Star here and fill in the form

Achieved

—————— LO-GO-GO-GO ——————

Design your
own logo here.

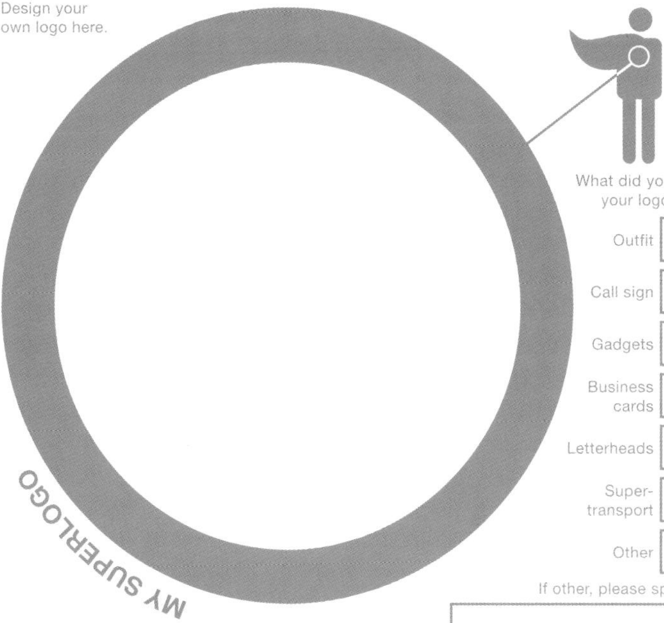

MY SUPERLOGO

What did you use
your logo for?

Outfit

Call sign

Gadgets

Business
cards

Letterheads

Super-
transport

Other

If other, please specify

Take a look at other logos down your main street. In the boxes
below, draw the three you think work the best and see if your
sidekick can identify the company they belong to.

Company?   Company?   Company?

Did you use
this power for...
GOOD? or
EVIL?

At the same time you could master these other **Ways**:
2: Choose Your Name • **17**: Choose Your Outfit • **48**: Choose a Calling Card
67: Select a Call Signal • **79**: Design Your Own Gadgets • **83**: Hand–Eye Skill

Control Your Temper

Emotions are powerful things. One might occasionally act irrationally out of intense feelings of love, but the trouble with anger is that it's far more likely to be destructive if given free rein. It isn't wrong to feel angry—it's a natural defense mechanism, enabling us to fight back against attack—but give in to it and you risk becoming what you hate.

Seeing Red

- Anger and frustration will make your heart rate, blood pressure, and adrenaline levels go up. If this energy is not given some sort of release, it could eventually explode—which may cause you to lash out at those around you—or implode, triggering self-destructive urges. There are more harmless ways to release this energy: playing sports; running; beating up a pillow; taking long, deep, relaxing breaths; dancing wildly like a lunatic; or letting out a long scream (these last two are best done in private).

- As a superhero, you're bound to be faced with people whose actions make you feel various degrees of moral outrage. Remember, though: you may be superhuman, but you are not a god. People will come to expect great things of you, but you will not always succeed. You must learn to deal with criticism, disappointment, guilt, and low self-esteem. Your enemy will know how to exploit these insecurities, but when you feel the anger boiling up, try to calm down by asking yourself questions that force you to look at things logically.

 Turning the tables: Nothing gets up a nasty bully's nose more than being ignored. When your enemy tries to provoke you into losing your temper, remain as calm and detached as you can, and you'll soon find the one getting their panties in a bunch is not you, but them.

Control Your Temper Form

Once you have mastered this **Way to Become a Superhero**, stick your Achieved Star here and fill in the form

☆ Achieved

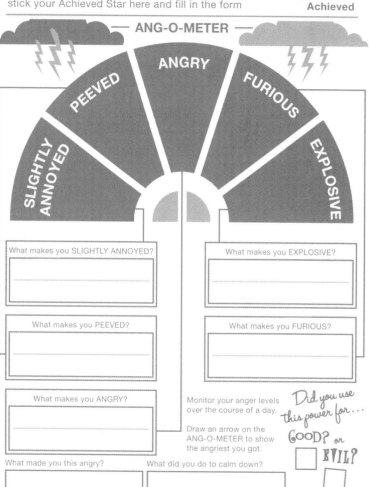

— ANG-O-METER —

ANGRY

PEEVED

FURIOUS

SLIGHTLY ANNOYED

EXPLOSIVE

What makes you SLIGHTLY ANNOYED?

What makes you PEEVED?

What makes you ANGRY?

What made you this angry?

What makes you EXPLOSIVE?

What makes you FURIOUS?

Monitor your anger levels over the course of a day.

Draw an arrow on the ANG-O-METER to show the angriest you got.

Did you use this power for...

GOOD? or
☐ EVIL?
☐

What did you do to calm down?

At the same time you could master these other **Ways**:
8: Kick Ass Humanely • 11: Groom Your Dark Side • 26: Know Your Weaknesses
70: Cope Under Pressure • 84: Resist Temptation • 101: Save the World from Yourself

My darling S,

Promise you'll take care tonight.
And stay away from kryptonite!

Lois xxx

Know Your Weaknesses

It'd be a real bummer if, having battled against all the odds to save humanity from some evil plan, rescuing hundreds of lives and defeating legions of your enemy's henchmen in the process, you were to be floored in the final confrontation with your nemesis thanks to your allergy to his or her cat. All superheroes suffer from some type of vulnerability, and it is good to discover what yours is before your nemesis does.

Follow the Leader

- Consider first what your strengths are and what defines you as a superhero. This can offer clues as to where your frailties lie, since it is often true that a superhero's weakness lies perilously close to the source of his or her strength (Superman's intolerance to fragments of rock from his home planet Krypton being a case in point). If, for example, you have extraordinary powers of hearing, there's a strong chance that very loud noises might be unbearable, even dangerous.

- List any personal issues that threaten your ability to do your job, be they emotional hang-ups, irrational fears, or physical inabilities. It can be hard to admit to one's own weaknesses. Ask someone who knows you well and whom you can trust to give you their honest opinion.

- Is there any protective item or equipment that might help you deal with your weakness? Put together an emergency pack containing first aid, survival items, and, crucially, anything that might counteract the effects of an attack on your Achilles heel.

 What's their kryptonite? Your nemesis may well have a fatal flaw too. Finding out what it is will give you a valuable advantage over him or her in a showdown of strength. Conduct the same sort of research on them to try to figure out what that weak spot might be.

Know Your Weaknesses Form

Once you have mastered this **Way to Become a Superhero**,
stick your Achieved Star here and fill in the form

Achieved

───── WEAK IN THE KNEES ─────

It's time to take a long, hard look at yourself and be brutally honest about your physical, mental,
and emotional weaknesses. To ensure you have the full picture, get a second opinion from your
sidekick—and encourage them to be brutally honest too!

DECLARATION OF WEAKNESSES

CLAUSE 101.5: I, THE UNDERSIGNED, PROMISE NOT TO GET ANNOYED,
OFFENDED, OR UPSET BY ANYTHING IN MY SIDEKICK'S ASSESSMENT

Signed _____ (Your name here)

YOUR VOLUNTARY DECLARATION	YOUR SIDEKICK'S VOLUNTARY DECLARATION
My weaknesses are . . .	His/her weaknesses are . . .

───── EMERGENCY PACK ─────

If your nemesis cunningly manages to use your weaknesses against
you, you should have an emergency pack ready to patch yourself up
and get you back on track. What kind of things would be helpful?

Item 1	Item 2	Item 3
Item 4	Item 5	Item 6
Item 7	Item 8	Item 9

At the same time you could master these other **Ways**:
13: Conquer Your Fears • **25**: Control Your Temper • **59**: Take Risks • **68**: Survive
Your Fatal Flaw • **70**: Cope Under Pressure • **101**: Save the World from Yourself

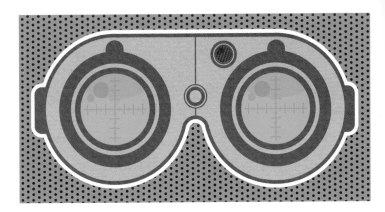

See in the Dark

It's not strictly true that eating carrots helps you to see in the dark, but dark green leafy vegetables as well as orange ones do provide vitamin A, which is especially good for healthy eyes. Still, you'll need to do a bit more than eat like a rabbit if you want better night vision. There are other ways . . .

For Your Eyes Only

- The retina at the back of the eye is made up of rod cells and cone cells. Cones detect color and rods detect movement, and so rods are the ones we need most when there's little or no light. There aren't any rod cells in the small area called the fovea right behind the pupil, so it's better to scan and use your peripheral vision to see in the dark than to try to focus on one direct spot.
- Practice your night vision in a room with a dimmer switch. Ask your sidekick to help by standing at the other side of the room and holding up pieces of paper on which symbols have been drawn. Try to read the symbols in different levels of lighting, starting with complete darkness and gradually turning the dimmer up until you can see all the symbols clearly. You should practice this regularly.
- It takes time for the eyes to adjust when plunged into darkness. Speed up this adjustment time by closing your eyes tightly for short periods before entering a dark place, and once in the dark, don't look directly at any light source, as this will make it harder to see. However, you could flash a light in your enemy's eyes to disable their night vision!

 Ninja-vision: Students of Ninjutsu are told to stay low in the dark. One of the reasons for this is that if you're lower than the people or objects you're trying to locate, you're at a better angle to spot them silhouetted against whatever light (e.g., moonlight) there is.

See in the Dark **Form**

Once you have mastered this **Way to Become a Superhero**, stick your Achieved Star here and fill in the form

Achieved

—— THINGS THAT GO BUMP IN THE NIGHT ——

Improving your night vision doesn't have to be all work, work, work. Here are some ways to make training fun.

MURDER IN THE DARK

YOU NEED: 4+ players • a large room that can be pitch-dark once the lights are off and that is safe to wander around in without getting hurt or breaking anything • small pieces of paper (one for each player) • a pen • a hat

HOW TO PLAY: Write "D" for "Detective" on one piece of paper, "M" for "Murderer" on another, and leave the rest blank. Fold the pieces up and throw them into a hat. Each player picks one out, but only the person who gets "D" reveals who they are. Everyone else's identity is secret. Those who pick blank pieces of paper are all potential victims/suspects.

The detective should leave the room, turning out the light as they go. Everyone else is free to move about in the dark. The murderer looks for a victim and, having found one, taps them sharply on the shoulder. That victim must fall to the floor, screaming as they "die." This is the detective's cue to reenter the room, turning the light back on.

The detective must now guess who the murderer is. If they guess correctly, the game is over and the detective wins. If they get it wrong, the murderer wins—or, if you're playing with a lot of people, add another round and let the murderer pick off a second victim in the dark, after which the detective makes another guess at who did it. You can keep doing this until there are only two survivors left in the room. At this point, if the detective guesses wrongly, the murderer has won.

How many games did you play in total? | 0 , 0

Did you win when you were the murderer? | y/n | How many victims did you "kill"? | 0 , 0

Did you win when you were the detective? | y/n | If yes, how many rounds did it take? | 0 , 0

How many times were you a victim? | 0 , 0 | How many times were you wrongly accused? | 0 , 0

NAVIGATION IN THE DARK

Can you navigate around your home without being able to see? Before you start, hide an apple or orange somewhere in every room. Your task is to retrieve these in the dark, so DON'T put them anywhere dangerous, like a cutlery drawer or oven.

You can do this task blindfolded or wait until nightfall and turn off the lights and close the curtains and blinds.

TIPS:

1. In the dark, distances can seem a lot bigger than they actually are.

2. Move slowly and carefully in case a chair has been left in the middle of the room by accident. You don't want to cause yourself an injury.

3. When it comes to stairs, you should crawl up them—but DO NOT attempt to climb down any stairs in the dark.

4. To play it extra safe, ask your sidekick to watch you (with a flashlight if necessary) and shout out warnings if you're in danger of hurting yourself or knocking something over.

How many apples/oranges did you manage to retrieve? | 0 , 0

How many times did you bump into something? | 0 , 0

Did you use this power for...
GOOD? or **EVIL?**

Did your sidekick have to help you? | y/n

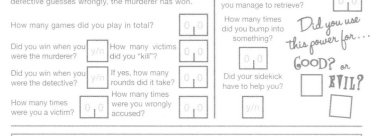

At the same time you could master these other **Ways:**
5: Super-Vision • 10: Stealth • 16: Sixth Sense • 34: Supersmell • 60: Save the World from the Undead • 62: Superhearing • 63: Observation Skills

Balance

All the other skills you add to your superphysical skills portfolio will be wasted if you can't stay on your feet. Gravity can be both friend and foe. It is much better to understand it than attempt to defy it.

Use the Force

- Every object has a center of gravity, where the weight on any side of that point is equal, keeping the object perfectly balanced. In humans, it lies somewhere below the belly button between your stomach and back when standing straight, but moves depending on your position. Stand in a relaxed but upright posture and feel where your center of gravity lies. Keeping your eyes fixed on a stationary point in front of you helps you maintain balance.
- Try standing on a bottom step with your feet apart and toes overlapping the edge. Close your eyes and gradually bring your feet together. Finally, stand on one leg and hold that position for as long as you can. Now try these positions again but sling a heavy bag over first one shoulder, then the other. Try holding the heavy bag at arm's length. If you can still find your center of balance, you're doing well.
- Juggling, ballet, tai chi, and yoga are great activities to help improve balance. At home, strengthen your stomach muscles with sit-ups and walk around with a book on your head. Also practice pirouetting: spin on one foot, keeping your eyes focused on one spot and whipping your head around as you rotate to find that spot quickly again.

Did you know . . . that our sense of balance relies on a system of canals in the inner ear? Sensory hair cells detect the movement of liquid in these canals, sending signals to the brain that tell our eyes and muscles what adjustments are needed to maintain balance.

Balance **Form**

Once you have mastered this **Way to Become a Superhero**,
stick your Achieved Star here and fill in the form

Achieved

──────── BALANCING ACTS ────────

Here are five tests to assess your current level of balancing skills. Try one attempt at each and record
your results. Practice them as often as you can to see if you can improve to superhero standards.

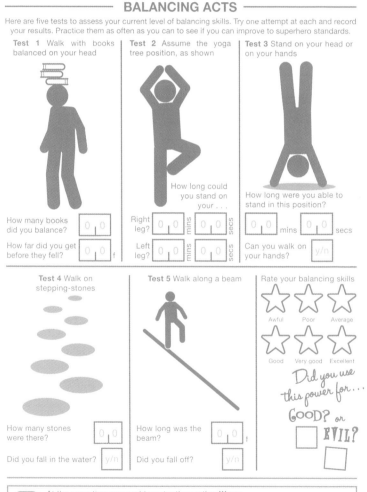

Test 1 Walk with books balanced on your head

How many books did you balance? `0 0`

How far did you get before they fell? `0 0` f

Test 2 Assume the yoga tree position, as shown

How long could you stand on your . . .

Right leg? `0 0` mins `0 0` secs

Left leg? `0 0` mins `0 0` secs

Test 3 Stand on your head or on your hands

How long were you able to stand in this position? `0 0` mins `0 0` secs

Can you walk on your hands? `y/n`

Test 4 Walk on stepping-stones

How many stones were there? `0 0`

Did you fall in the water? `y/n`

Test 5 Walk along a beam

How long was the beam? `0 0` f

Did you fall off? `y/n`

Rate your balancing skills

Awful   Poor   Average

Good   Very good   Excellent

Did you use this power for . . .

GOOD? or **EVIL?**

At the same time you could master these other **Ways**:
10: Stealth • **42**: Strike a Superhero Pose • **43**: Invisibility • **51**: Jump High
66: Agility • **69**: Kung-Fu Master • **83**: Hand–Eye Skill

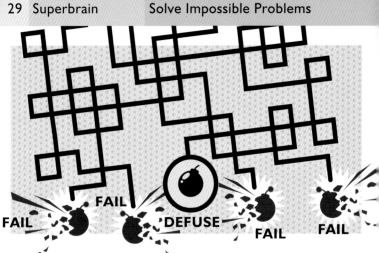

Solve Impossible Problems

You're in a sewer, standing in front of a timer that gives you ten minutes in which to evacuate the city or defuse Bogman's super swamp bomb. It will take him only five minutes to get back down the sewer with the president as hostage and escape in his wasteship. What a stinker! As a fully fledged superbeing, you'll face problems like this on a routine basis. Start brain-training now so when it comes to the crunch you can save the day, rescue the hostage, and catch the fiend without even breaking a sweat.

Crunch Time

- Problems come in all shapes and sizes. Start by looking at the facts. Examine every dimension of the problem so you don't mess up by not noticing some major obstacle, like the trip wires around the bomb, or some major opportunity, like the "Cancel" button on the timer panel.
- When analyzing the problem, ask yourself questions like: How much time is there? Can I buy more time? What is my priority? What tools do I need? Do I have them or can I adapt them from what's around me?
- Problems of this magnitude may require all manner of mental skills: intelligence can't be measured simply by verbal and mathematical ability. There are plenty of IQ tests available online to get you doing mental gymnastics, but you can start with the challenges set out on the opposite page (don't worry—answers are in the back).
- To prepare yourself for solving huge puzzles under pressure, buy the biggest jigsaw puzzle you can find and set a time limit for completion.

Action plan: Every action has a consequence, so before you rush in to fix things, consider the possible consequences of each of your actions. Think through the whole maneuver step by step, to ensure that you are always moving closer to your goal, not farther away.

Solve Impossible Problems **Form**

Once you have mastered this **Way to Become a Superhero**, stick your Achieved Star here and fill in the form

Achieved

———— BRAIN TRAIN ————

Here are seven brainteasers for you to solve. Some are easier than others. If you can answer them all correctly, you're well on your way to becoming a supersolver of impossible problems. If you can solve them all correctly in less than ten minutes, you're already there.

1. Brainiac-Boy, who is twelve years old, is four times as old as his sister, Captain Tantrum. How old will Brainiac-Boy be when he is twice as old as his sister?   `0 , 0`

2. If **24 H in a D = 24 HOURS IN A DAY**, what are the following:

   i) **60 S in a M**   ii) **12 D of C**

   iii) **101 W to B a S**   iv) **3 B M (S H T R)**

   | i | ii |
   | iii | iv |

3. Which number should come next in the series?

   1 – 2 – 4 – 7 – 11 – 16 – 22 – 29 – 37 –   `0 , 0`

4. Which larger shape would be made if the two sections are fitted together?

   Your answer here `[ ]`

   i.   ii.   iii.   iv.

5. What number is 1/4 of 1/2 of 1/5 of 400?   `0 , 0`

6. If BD = 1, HM = 4 and KT = 8, what is VY?   `0 , 0`

7. You're on your way home after a mission in your supervehicle. You have 100 mi to travel and you are traveling at 125 mi/hour, but your fuel tank is leaking. You had 7 gallons of fuel before you set off and you know you can do 25 mi per gallon, but you're leaking a gallon every 16 mins.

Will you have enough fuel to get home? `y/n`

SCORE `/ 10`   TIME `0 , 0` mins `0 , 0` secs

Answers at the back of the book.

———— MADE UP ————

For the second part of your test, you'll need a construction set—it could be a Lego one, any kind of model-building kit, or even an origami set. Your task is to try to build the model pictured on the box/cover WITHOUT referring to the instructions. You must figure out how to put it together from the finished picture alone.

What did you attempt to build?

`[            ]` Did you succeed? `y/n`

If yes, how long did it take to complete?

`0 , 0` hrs `0 , 0` mins `0 , 0` secs

How many times, if at all, did you peek at the instructions? `0 , 0`

How did it compare with the picture on the box? Did it look . . .

. . . awful—completely different? `y/n`

. . . almost the same? `y/n`

. . . good—but completely different? `y/n`

. . . identical? `y/n`

Did you use this power for . . .
GOOD? or **EVIL?** `[ ]`

At the same time you could master these other **Ways**:
7: Decipher Devious Riddles • **21**: Dexterity • **39**: Speed • **41**: Become a Science Genius
59: Take Risks • **70**: Cope Under Pressure • **88**: Acquire Specialist Knowledge

Save the World from Alien Attack

When the little green men finally show up on our beloved planet, it's best to be prepared for the worst. If we're lucky they'll be the sort of ETs who take us for sky-rides on bicycles. If so, then your job will be to act as Earth's ambassador and welcome them. If they have less sociable activities in mind, you will have to step up as Earth's protector.

ET Go Home!

- Just because you can't see them doesn't mean they're not here. Aliens may have shape-shifting powers so they can blend into society. Use your observation skills to detect subtle signs of unhuman behavior.
- Don't immediately assume alien visitors are hostile. You don't want to ruin a beautiful friendship before it's had a chance to blossom. Observe them, particularly the way they interact. If you can only communicate with them, you might be able to avoid a confrontation.
- Even if they do prove hostile, try to find out what the ETs want. Maybe their own planet can no longer support them, or they're under threat from other aliens. Perhaps you can solve these problems together. Of course they may just be sadistic scum intent on kicking our asses, in which case feel free to teach them all you know on that subject.
- No one's invincible, not even the meanest, greenest ETs. When the army's conventional weapons prove useless, it'll be up to you to find their weak spot. In the meantime, though, make sure the civilian population is protected. The army and police can help you with this.

 One move and I'll banana you: In H. G. Wells's *The War of the Worlds*, it was bacteria in the air that proved the aliens' undoing; in *Mars Attacks*, it was the music of Slim Whitman. That's pretty specific. In other words, be prepared to try anything against them, no matter how ridiculous.

Save the World . . .
from Alien Attack **Form**

Once you have mastered this **Way to Become a Superhero**,
stick your Achieved Star here and fill in the form

Achieved

ALIENS

— KNOW YOUR ENEMY —

Aliens are masters of disguise, so you need to keep your internal radar on full
alert if you're to detect one in our midst. Is there anyone you already suspect
of being an ET? Create a profile on them below.

Name of alien suspect

Enemy weaknesses

Which of the following telltale signs do they exhibit?

Bizarre dress sense	y/n
Twisted sense of humor	y/n
Secretive nature	y/n

Physical defect(s)	y/n
Strange dietary habits	y/n
Superhuman powers	y/n

Enemy strengths

Is your alien suspect likely to be hostile? Do they . . .

. . . carry any weapons? y/n   . . . complain about human behavior? y/n

. . . have a violent temper? y/n   . . . complain about overpopulation? y/n

YOU NEED A PLAN OF ACTION. WILL YOU . . .	Explain how you will carry out your plan below
. . . interrogate your suspect? y/n	
. . . try to expose your suspect? y/n	
. . . neutralize your suspect? y/n	
. . . report your suspect? y/n	
. . . join your suspect? y/n	

Place a photo of
your alien suspect here

*Did you use
this power for . . .*
GOOD? or
EVIL?

At the same time you could master these other **Ways**:
33: Anticipate Your Enemy's Next Move • **63**: Observation Skills
72: Speak a Hundred Languages • **73**: Create a Force Field • **92**: Telepathy

Identify Your Nemesis

You may not know it, but somewhere out there is a person whose destiny is tied inextricably to your own. And we're not talking about The One, as in the person you'll fall in love with and live with happily ever after. Well, not quite. There's little happiness in this relationship, yet you may feel an odd, irresistible attraction to them . . .

Takes One to Know One

- The thing about a nemesis, as opposed to other regular types of enemy, is that you'll feel some sort of connection with them. While you may hate them and all they stand for, when you dig deep you'll recognize something of yourself in them. This makes them hard to spot.
- Make a list of suspects. Think of everyone you know—is there anyone to whom you feel strangely drawn, who seems to take an unnerving interest in you but for whom you feel both attraction and revulsion in equal measure? Is there anyone you want both to impress and to destroy?
- To narrow down your list, examine each suspect for motives either one of you may have for harboring a secret but intensifying desire to confront the other in a showdown. Ex–best friends are a good place to start. No one should escape the finger of suspicion, not even your sidekick.
- Your nemesis will be like the goddess so named in classical mythology: an embodiment of retribution and punishment. For some reason, known or unknown, the person you're looking for will be hell-bent on kicking your ass, because they truly believe you deserve it.

Would like to meet: If you can't identify your nemesis, you may have to take a more direct approach and advertise for one. Place your ad somewhere like-minded people will see it, and make sure you spend plenty of time getting to know him/her before you make your mind up.

Identify Your Nemesis **Form**

Once you have mastered this **Way to Become a Superhero**,
stick your Achieved Star here and fill in the form

☆ **Achieved**

Nemesis Assessment

Hitting you ☐ ☐ ☐

PART 1—IDENTIFICATION: List your
top three suspects below.

Threatening
your life ☐ ☐ ☐

1.

Hurting someone
you love ☐ ☐ ☐

2.

Which suspect
scored highest? [60] [60] [60]

YOU'VE FOUND YOUR NEMESIS!

3.

On a scale of 0–10, rate . . .

    1   2   3

PART 2—PROFILE:
Name your nemesis

. . . how much you
hate each suspect. [10] [10] [10]

. . . how much you
think each suspect [10] [10] [10]
hates you.

How do you know them?

. . . how much you
have in common [10] [10] [10]
with each of them.

List their possible motives for hating you

Add up
your suspects'
scores so far: [30] [30] [30]

Which of your 3 suspects are guilty of the
following crimes against you? For every
check in their column, add 5 points to the
suspects' total score

List their most irritating
characteristics below

*Did you use
this knowledge
for . . .*

    1   2   3

Humiliating
you ☐ ☐ ☐

GOOD? *or*

☐ **EVIL?**

Stealing from
you ☐ ☐ ☐

☐

Cheating you ☐ ☐ ☐

At the same time you could master these other **Ways:**
1: Discover Your Alter Ego • **4**: Have a Twisted Backstory • **33**: Anticipate Your Enemy's
Next Move • **71**: Trace Your Superhero Origins • **89**: Know When Someone's Lying

Get a Villainous Chair

Getting your first villainous chair is something of a rite of passage in the criminal underworld. It isn't just a place to park your behind, it's a symbol of power. It's from here that you'll come up with your most dastardly plots, order your minions to do your dirty work for you, and laugh at your enemies.

Seat of Power

- You may find suitable chair designs in stores, but as you've no doubt discovered en route to becoming an evil mastermind, if you want something done properly, the only way is to do it yourself. Any chair can become villainous with a bit of ingenious bling.
- Big is best. This isn't simply to make your chair comfortable (though being able to put your feet up is nice), but to create a dramatic effect. Your chair should also provide a protective shell around you.
- The precise style of your chair should depend on the evil identity you've assumed. A leopard-skin pattern isn't to everyone's taste, but if you model yourself on the evil, exotic jungle chief type, then this might be the fabric for you. Black is the norm, but don't feel you have to stick with this. What's important is that you dominate from your chair—your chair mustn't dominate you. No fluorescent pink.
- What accessories might come in handy? Somewhere to conceal your weapon? A control panel with some buttons to play around with? A cup-holder for your coffee and a drawer for your remote controls, wigs, and fake IDs? Make sure you incorporate them in your design.

 Catteries included: Some chairs come with the white cat accessory. The delightful contrast of pure white against the darkness of evil has made it a top choice. But don't feel limited to white, or even a cat. Choose your own cuddly companion, the cuter the better.

Get a Villainous Chair **Form**

Once you have mastered this **Way to Become an Evil Genius**,
stick your Achieved Star here and fill in the form

Achieved

——————————————— **SIT ON IT** ———————————————

Every supervillain should have an impressive seat of power from which they can comfortably and
securely make their plans for world domination. Find an old chair and bling it up, installing items
and gadgets fit for an evil genius.

Technical specifications

Color   Material

Dimensions (in inches)   0 0 0 X 0 0 0 X 0 0 0

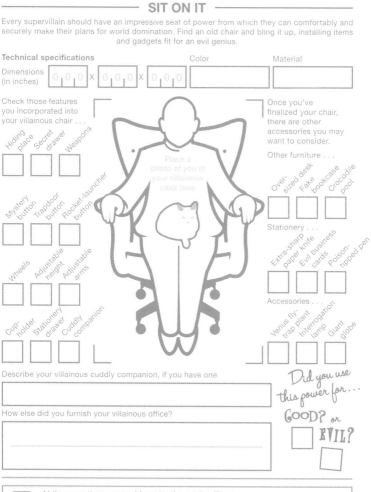

Check those features you incorporated into your villainous chair . . .

Hiding place   Secret drawer   Weapons

Mystery button   Trapdoor button   Rocket-launcher button

Wheels   Adjustable height   Adjustable arms

Cup-holder   Stationery drawer   Cuddly companion

Place a photo of you in your villainous chair here

Once you've finalized your chair, there are other accessories you may want to consider.

Other furniture . . .

Over-sized desk   Fake bookcase   Crocodile pool

Stationery . . .

Extra-sharp paper knife   Evil business cards   Poison-tipped pen

Accessories . . .

Venus fly-trap plant   Interrogation lamp   Giant globe

Describe your villainous cuddly companion, if you have one

How else did you furnish your villainous office?

Did you use this power for...

GOOD? or

EVIL?

At the same time you could master these other **Ways**:
11: Groom Your Dark Side • **23**: Plan for World Domination • **37**: Train Your Superpet
79: Design Your Own Gadgets • **97**: Know What's Happening Everywhere

Anticipate Your Enemy's Next Move

On those quiet days when the sun is out, the birds are singing and all seems well with the world, don't imagine you can forget your superhero cares and go and frolic outside with your friends. It is precisely those quiet days when you can be sure your nemesis is hardest at work, plotting and laying down plans, and if you listen hard enough, you might just pick up on something.

Checkmate

- Playing chess provides excellent training, as it's vital to anticipate your opponent's next move to have any hope of winning the game. Very often their move will depend on yours, so you have to follow through the consequences in your head before you commit to a move. Your opponent shouldn't be able to do anything that takes you by surprise.
- It's much easier to predict what someone will do if you know them well. Make profiles on all your enemies, adding to them every time you learn something new. Try to establish any patterns in their behavior.
- Spying is a risky business but the rewards can make it worthwhile. Of course you need to know where to find your enemy (or their associates), and it may be a while before you catch them doing or saying something incriminating. Train by spying on your sidekick. The days leading up to Christmas or your birthday are a good time, as you can make it your mission to find out what they plan to buy you (a closely guarded secret). Eavesdrop on them, tail them when they go out, search for hard evidence (e.g., shopping lists), and be on high alert for clues in their conversation.

I spy with my supereye . . . If your superpowers aren't up to scratch yet, take a spy kit with you on missions; e.g., a small camera (if it's on your cell, be sure to turn the phone to silent!), a newspaper with eye holes cut out, a periscope for seeing around corners, a fake ID, etc.

Anticipate Your Enemy's . . .
Next Move **Form**

Once you have mastered this **Way to Become a Superhero**,
stick your Achieved Star here and fill in the form

Achieved

JUST FOR KICKS

Penalty shoot-outs are all about anticipating your opponent's next move. It's a mind game between goalie and penalty-taker. Challenge your sidekick to a super shoot-out—first to five—each taking a turn as goalie and a turn as penalty kicker. Check successful penalties and cross missed ones.

> Your name here

① ② ③ ④ ⑤ ⑥ ⑦

> Your opponent's name here

① ② ③ ④ ⑤ ⑥ ⑦

On the diagram below mark on the net where your penalties ended up

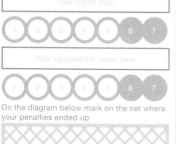

SAVED

REMATCH?

> Your name here

① ② ③ ④ ⑤ ⑥ ⑦

> Your opponent's name here

① ② ③ ④ ⑤ ⑥ ⑦

Rate your penalty-taking skills [ ] / 10   Rate your penalty-saving skills [ ] / 10

SECOND-CHESSING

After your penalty shoot-out competition, it's time to go mental and test your ability to predict your opponent's next move in a chess tournament. Make it a best out of three so that you have a chance to study your opponent's preferred strategy and stay one step ahead of the game.

GAME 1 Who won?

[ ]

How long did it take? [0 0] hrs [0 0] mins [0 0] secs

How many pieces did . . .

. . . you take? [0 0]   . . . your opponent take? [0 0]

GAME 2 Who won?

[ ]

How long did it take? [0 0] hrs [0 0] mins [0 0] secs

How many pieces did . . .

. . . you take? [0 0]   . . . your opponent take? [0 0]

GAME 3 Who won?

[ ]

How long did it take? [0 0] hrs [0 0] mins [0 0] secs

How many pieces did . . .

. . . you take? [0 0]   . . . your opponent take? [0 0]

Rate your chess-playing skills

Did you use this power for . . .

☆ Awful ☆ Poor ☆ Average

☆ Good ☆ Very good ☆ Excellent

GOOD? *or* [ ]

EVIL? [ ]

At the same time you could master these other **Ways**:
27: See in the Dark • **50**: Second Sight • **74**: Identify and Interpret Clues • **92**: Telepathy
95: Build a Network of Contacts • **97**: Know What's Happening Everywhere

Supersmell

It's time to hone your hooter, cultivate your nasal cavities, and augment your olfactory epithelium. A sharp schnozz can alert you to many dangers in good time to do something about them.

A Nose That Knows

- The science of smell remains one of the great mysteries of human biology. We know the olfactory epithelium contains the cells that detect smells—over 10,000 of them—and that these cells trigger signals in the olfactory nerve that are sent to the brain, but we don't know how. A dog can smell over a million smells with each nostril. If you want to be superhuman, you need to smell like a dog.
- Ask your sidekick to gather together a collection of items that vary in pungency, from powerful-smelling things like garlic, bacon, and coffee to delicate scents like apple, pencil shavings, and grass. Ask them to put each item in a plastic cup and then blindfold you. Without peeping at or touching the items, try to figure out what they are.
- Now ask your sidekick to mix two or three of the items together and see if you can distinguish each individual smell in the mix.
- Write numbers 1–5 on the bottom of five plastic cups. Fill each cup halfway with water, then add one drop of perfume to cup 1, two to cup 2, and so on. Move the cups around so you don't know which is which. Now sniff each in turn and try to reorder them according to the strength of the smell. Check the numbers afterward to see if you were right.

Smell hell: It's not just things you need to be able to sniff out, but people. Ask five friends to offer you a top they've worn that hasn't been washed yet. With your blindfold on, see if you can match the top to the person. Don't sniff too deeply in case you become asphyxiated!

Supersmell **Form**

Once you have mastered this **Way to Become a Superhero**, stick your Achieved Star here and fill in the form

☆ **Achieved**

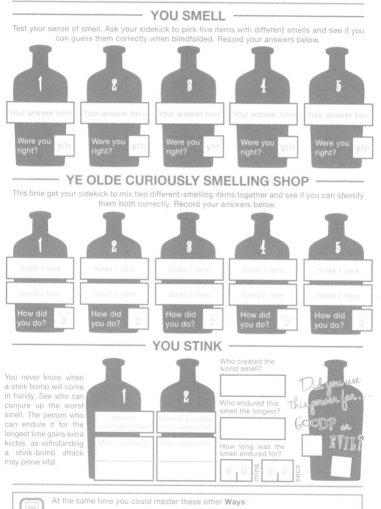

YOU SMELL

Test your sense of smell. Ask your sidekick to pick five items with different smells and see if you can guess them correctly when blindfolded. Record your answers below.

1 Your answer here — Were you right? y/n

2 Your answer here — Were you right? y/n

3 Your answer here — Were you right? y/n

4 Your answer here — Were you right? y/n

5 Your answer here — Were you right? y/n

YE OLDE CURIOUSLY SMELLING SHOP

This time get your sidekick to mix two different-smelling items together and see if you can identify them both correctly. Record your answers below.

1 Smell 1 here / Smell 2 here — How did you do?

2 Smell 1 here / Smell 2 here — How did you do?

3 Smell 1 here / Smell 2 here — How did you do?

4 Smell 1 here / Smell 2 here — How did you do?

5 Smell 1 here / Smell 2 here — How did you do?

YOU STINK

You never know when a stink bomb will come in handy. See who can conjure up the worst smell. The person who can endure it for the longest time gains extra kudos, as withstanding a stink-bomb attack may prove vital.

1 Name of your concoction / Main ingredients

2 Name of your sidekick's concoction / Main ingredients

Who created the worst smell?

Who endured this smell the longest?

How long was the smell endured for?
0 0 mins 0 0 secs

Did you use this power for... GOOD? or EVIL?

At the same time you could master these other **Ways**:
5: Super-Vision • 62: Superhearing • 89: Know When Someone's Lying

Identify Opportunities to Help

Superheroes must never adopt a fine-dining attitude to doing good, pursuing only the most dastardly foes and feasting on only the most deluxe evil. All sorts of bad things happen all the time, and your journey toward superhero status will require you to take on the less glamorous challenges in order to prepare for supervillains or disasters on a global scale.

Serve Them Right

- You'll find more than enough fodder if you check the Internet or papers for bad news, but firsthand observation alone should alert you to opportunities to practice superheroism. Spend a day on field research, recording each time you see someone in need of assistance. Also note: 1) what's at stake (e.g., someone's health, damage to an object); 2) your ability to help, or, if unable to help, what skills or resources you lack. The latter will provide you with homework.
- How do you prioritize when there's so much good to do? Come up with a rating system for your "what's at stake" column. Life is about the most valuable thing we have, so saving it is definitely a five-star deed. Saving someone's sandwich from being run over comes rather lower in the rating system. In fact, if an attempt to save the sandwich could put other lives in danger, you really need to think again.
- Ever said, "Well, that's my good deed for the day"? Then you should be aiming higher. Tomorrow do one good deed, the next day two, then three, and so on until doing good becomes a way of life.

 Prevention's better than cure: You're not just looking for people/animals in distress; you're looking to stop bad things from happening before they do. This doesn't mean becoming some health and safety freak, but it does mean being able to read the signs.

Identify Opportunities to Help **Form**

Once you have mastered this **Way to Become a Superhero**, stick your Achieved Star here and fill in the form

Achieved

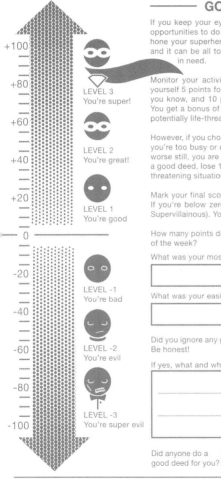

+100
+80

LEVEL 3
You're super!

+60

LEVEL 2
You're great!

+40

+20

LEVEL 1
You're good

0

-20

LEVEL -1
You're bad

-40

LEVEL -2
You're evil

-60

-80

LEVEL -3
You're super evil

-100

———— GOOD FOR YOU! ————

If you keep your eyes open you'll find there are plenty of opportunities to do good deeds every day. It takes time to hone your superhero senses to be on constant help alert, and it can be all too easy to turn a blind eye to someone in need.

Monitor your activity over the course of a week. Award yourself 5 points for every good deed you do for someone you know, and 10 points for those you do for a stranger. You get a bonus of 50 points if you help someone out of a potentially life-threatening situation.

However, if you choose to ignore someone in need because you're too busy or can't be bothered, you lose 5 points. If, worse still, you are the cause of someone being in need of a good deed, lose 10 points. If you ignore a potentially life-threatening situation, lose 50 points.

Mark your final score on the chart at the end of the week. If you're below zero, you're in the wrong section (turn to Supervillainous). Your target is 100 points.

How many points did you have at the end of the week?   `0 , 0 , 0`

What was your most worthy good deed?

What was your easiest good deed?

Did you ignore any good deeds that needed doing? Be honest!   `y/n`

If yes, what and why?

Did anyone do a good deed for you? `y/n`   If yes, do you think they could be a superhero too? `y/n`

At the same time you could master these other **Ways**:
19: Know Whom to Save First • **36**: Be in Two Places at Once • **49**: Hone Your Moral Compass • **63**: Observation Skills • **97**: Know What's Happening Everywhere

HERE | THERE
& EVERYWHERE!

Be in Two Places at Once

Unless you have an identical twin or you're willing to offer yourself as a human guinea pig to Dolly the sheep's genetic scientist pals, this will be hard. You have to be cunning; you have to be devious. You have to find your doppelgänger.

Double Vision

- Think about the sort of scenarios where two of you would be useful. It could be to protect your civilian identity, in case you have something vital to do in your normal life as well as answering a call for help. If it's to help you multitask, so you can respond to two emergencies at the same time, you're in trouble. You'll need someone who not only looks, talks, and acts like you, but kicks ass like you too.
- If your sidekick's out of the question, consider your other friends. Is there anyone who, with the help of hair and makeup, could pass themselves off as you? They have to know you really well and be relied on not to butt in to what you're up to while they're pretending to be you.
- Do a survey among the people who know you best, asking them about your habits, both annoying and cute, and any notable physical or verbal mannerisms. You will probably discover things about yourself that you didn't know. Use this research as a basis for training your body double.
- Put potential candidates to the test, starting with something easy, like impersonating you on the phone. If they can do this, try something harder, like making them go and say hello to your friend's mom.

The perfect alibi: If you're of a supervillainous bent, a body double is a great way of avoiding the pointing finger of suspicion. How could you be guilty of the dastardly deed if at the time it was committed someone saw you in a store trying on a pair of sneakers?

Be in Two Places at Once **Form**

Once you have mastered this **Way to Become a Superhero**, stick your Achieved Star here and fill in the form

Achieved

——— NOW YOU SEE ME . . . ———

If you have an identical twin, this **Way to Become a Superhero** will be supereasy. If not, you'll have to find someone you can easily mold in your own image. They'll need a comprehensive makeover and some one-to-one tuition in being you.

Whom did you pick to be your body double?

After their makeover and training, rate them on . . .

. . . similarity of appearance | 10

. . . similarity of voice | 10

Rate how much they look like you before their makeover | 10

. . . similarity of kick-ass abilities | 10

. . . similarity of mannerisms | 10

Send your body double on a mission to try to fool people.

What was the mission you gave them?

Did they manage to fool anyone? | y/n

If yes, who?

Place a photo of you here

Place a photo of your doppelgänger in the same pose here

What did you do while your body double was out being you?

Rate the likeness of the two photos | 10

——— BORDER CONTROL ———

It's possible to be physically in two different places at the same time—you just have to be standing in the right place. Go to the border of your county and put a foot over into the next county and—presto!—you've done it. You could even do this between countries.

Did you use this power for . . . **GOOD?** or **EVIL?**

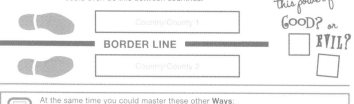

Country/County 1

BORDER LINE

Country/County 2

At the same time you could master these other **Ways**:
20: Learn to Multitask • **29**: Solve Impossible Problems • **47**: Master of Illusion
63: Observation Skills • **92**: Telepathy • **97**: Know What's Happening Everywhere

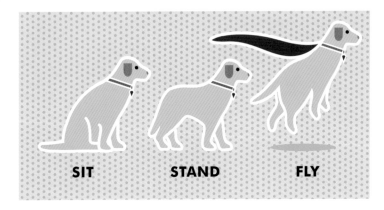

SIT   **STAND**   **FLY**

Train Your Superpet

It's said that dogs are man's best friend, but who is a superhuman's best friend? That's up to you. If you don't have a pet, you'll have to adopt a wild creature or secretly borrow a friend's pet. But remember, you won't get far with superpet training unless you learn to understand each other first.

Sit! Fetch! Kill!

- Spend time observing your superpet, following the guidelines in **Way to Become a Superhero** No. 22. It's vital to build up a relationship of complete trust between you.
- Identify your pet's strengths and weaknesses. What skills do they possess that could come in handy? What character flaws could jeopardize a mission? Dogs—at least the obedient ones—can be superheroes all on their own; anyone who's seen *Lassie* or *Benji* knows that. Cats can be trickier to train, as they tend to operate on their own terms. Gerbils, budgies, and fish may all appear a little more limited, but don't overlook their great spy potential.
- Make a list of the sort of tasks your superpet needs to do and create a training plan. This might include: fetching things, delivering messages, sniffing out things, acting as a diversion, getting into places you can't fit or reach, scaring people (difficult with a fish), and, let's not forget, providing comfort when everything's gone wrong. Design tests to help them perform more complex tasks, like pushing buttons. Would your superpet benefit from any gadgets you might be able to make for them?

 Pet name: Your superpet may not appreciate being dressed up in a fancy costume, and in any case this could impede their movement and spy potential. Still, for the purpose of team-building, you should at least give them an alter-ego name and a corner of your base to nap in.

Train Your Superpet **Form**

Once you have mastered this **Way to Become a Superhero**, stick your Achieved Star here and fill in the form

☆ **Achieved**

ANIMAL MAGIC

Write the name of your superpet here

What type of animal is he/she?

Rate your ability to understand your superpet `/10`

Rate your superpet's ability to understand you `/10`

Rate his/her willingness to obey your commands `/10`

Does your superpet have any special skills? `y/n`

If yes, place pictures of them performing those skills below. If no, teach them three useful tricks.

Place a photo of skill 1 here

Write the skill here

Place a photo of skill 2 here

Write the skill here

Place a photo of skill 3 here

Write the skill here

CAN YOUR SUPERPET . . .

. . . fetch things? `y/n`

. . . push buttons? `y/n`

. . . smell better than you can? `y/n`

. . . fly? `y/n`

. . . open doors? `y/n`

. . . deliver secret messages? `y/n`

. . . see better than you can? `y/n`

. . . swim? `y/n`

. . . open windows? `y/n`

. . . spy for you? `y/n`

. . . hear better than you can? `y/n`

. . . defend you against attack? `y/n`

. . . alert you to danger? `y/n`

. . . run faster than you can? `y/n`

Did you use this power for . . .

GOOD? or

EVIL?

Name your superpet's three main weaknesses

Is your superpet your best friend? `y/n`

Has he/she ever saved your life? `y/n`

Rate your super-pet's superpowers `/10`

At the same time you could master these other **Ways**:
9: Select a Sidekick • **10**: Stealth • **22**: Communicate with Animals
63: Observation Skills • **79**: Design Your Own Gadgets • **99**: Gather a Superteam

HELP WANTED
ARE YOU EVIL? BAD TO THE BONE?
HELL-BENT ON DESTRUCTION AND
SEEKING A CHANGE OF DIRECTION?
THEN WE NEED YOU . . .
Apply within

Assemble Your Armies of Darkness

There's a lot of day-to-day dirty work involved in any plan for world domination or mass destruction, and there's absolutely no reason why you should be the one to do it. Finding suitable henchmen to carry out your sinister activities can be a challenge, though.

Down, but Not Out

- Zombies, mutants, flying monkeys, werewolves—they're great if you want to scare your victims witless and create anarchy, but keeping such dangerous and unpredictable creatures in check can be tricky. You'll probably have to allow them to indulge their nasty appetites from time to time or else you'll need to possess the black magic to control them.
- Mindless thugs provide handy muscle and they don't tend to ask many questions. For more highly skilled soldiers, recruit some ninjas.
- The deluxe option is robots, but they're expensive and it takes time to build up an army. AI also has a nasty habit of acquiring a mind of its own. Aliens are a good alternative and often come with very tasty technology and unique weaponry. However, they'll probably have high demands. You may even have to consider power-sharing.
- Sometimes you need people with brains, but you'll have to find ways to keep them happy and occupied so they don't get any funny ideas above their station. Computer hackers and scientists are safe so long as you go for the really geeky ones who are delighted just to be given challenges but have little ambition beyond their field of expertise.

 Takes one to know one: Use other villains or crooked businessmen, politicians, and cops with care. These shady characters can open doors for you but are the least trustworthy. So employ them sparingly, pay them well, and never let them in on your master plan.

Assemble Your Armies of Darkness **Form**

Once you have mastered this **Way to Become an Evil Genius**, stick your Achieved Star here and fill in the form

Achieved

SEAT OF POWER

What sort of personnel will you recruit into your evil army? Think about the different areas of expertise you need and the sort of person (human or otherwise) best suited to the role. You might want to name someone specific for the senior jobs (feel free to poach some other famous villains' henchmen), or you can just name a species or group, like "zombies" (great cannon fodder) or "ninjas" (perfect for a S.W.A.T. team). Have fun!

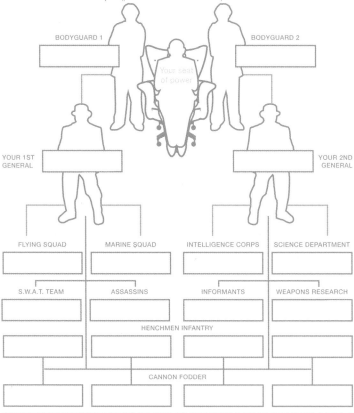

BODYGUARD 1

BODYGUARD 2

Your seat of power

YOUR 1ST GENERAL

YOUR 2ND GENERAL

FLYING SQUAD

MARINE SQUAD

INTELLIGENCE CORPS

SCIENCE DEPARTMENT

S.W.A.T. TEAM

ASSASSINS

INFORMANTS

WEAPONS RESEARCH

HENCHMEN INFANTRY

CANNON FODDER

At the same time you could master these other **Ways**:
22: Communicate with Animals • **23**: Plan for World Domination • **47**: Master of Illusion
69: Kung-Fu Master • **94**: Talk to Computers • **100**: Devise Your Villainous Comeback

Speed

Have you ever stood on the pavement when something really fast drives past and felt a gust of air on your face, perhaps even strong enough to push you back a step? Well, that's nothing compared to the speeds you need to achieve. You should be aiming to create tornado-strength winds.

Pull a Fast One

- The obvious way to train for this superpower is to run regularly—and that doesn't mean a leisurely jog to the park, unless this is a warm-up for the sprinting you're going to do when you get there. Warming up your muscles with some gentle stretching exercises at the start of a serious training session is important, though—it helps prevent injuries.
- When you're sprinting, you need to think about your arms as well as your legs. Try to keep your body relaxed—not so relaxed you're all floppy, but not tensed up so that you become rigid and inflexible. Keep your chin tucked in and your eyes fixed on a spot a little way in front of you. Your foot wants to strike the ground lightly and under your center of gravity—your hips. You'll know when you've broken the sound barrier, as you'll probably create an explosive sonic boom.
- When it comes to physical prowess, there's nothing like a bit of healthy competition to bring out the best in you, so challenge friends to a sprint. Also make sure your sidekick helps you train by timing your laps and counting how many strides you manage in a minute. It's the only way to measure your improvement accurately.

The path of most resistance: Practice running up hills. You'll have to work harder, lift your knees higher, and lean forward into the run. This will make running on flat ground feel so much easier, and help you to go from static to high speed so much more quickly.

Speed **Form**

Once you have mastered this **Way to Become a Superhero**,
stick your Achieved Star here and fill in the form

☆ **Achieved**

THE NEED FOR SPEED

There's no such thing as a sluggish superhero. See how fast you can go. A bit of competition is healthy and will bring out the best in you, so get your friends involved.

Running—Race your friends over a set distance.

Distance
| 0 | 0 | 0 | 0 | yards ➡

How many took part in the race? | 0 | 0 |

Who won the race?

Your time
| 0 | 0 | mins | 0 | 0 | secs

Swimming—Race your friends over a set distance.

Distance
| 0 | 0 | laps ➡

How many took part in the race? | 0 | 0 |

Who won the race?

Your time
| 0 | 0 | mins | 0 | 0 | secs

Cycling—Race your friends over a set distance.

Distance
| 0 | 0 | 0 | mi ➡

How many took part in the race? | 0 | 0 |

Who won the race?

Your time
| 0 | 0 | mins | 0 | 0 | secs

Which are you best at?

Running   Swimming   Cycling

□   □   □

What else can you do superfast?

Complete the sentence to describe yourself:
I'm faster than . . . (e.g., a speeding bullet)

Did you use this power for . . .
GOOD? □ or
EVIL? □

At the same time you could master these other **Ways**:
6: Stamina • **36**: Be in Two Places at Once • **66**: Agility • **76**: Devise an Escape Plan
91: Design Your Supertransport

Understand Body Language

Being able to read other people's physical behavior will help you to understand them better, which could be vital if their intentions are in doubt. And being more aware of the power of body language will help you use yours to become a better and more powerful communicator.

Silent Clues

- Eye contact, facial expression, the space you use, posture, gesture, tone, touch, intensity, timing—these are all part of the way we communicate, though we may not consciously control them. Can you think of any more ways? Watch others closely for clues and cues to their feelings.
- Ask your sidekick to secretly film you in conversation with someone you like and someone you don't (if secrecy's not possible you'll need to invent some sort of "research" purpose for the recording). Afterward, watch the two films with the sound turned off, and try to read the non-verbal conversations going on. How do they compare to the verbal ones? What is really being said?
- Write down a list of words to describe someone's feelings or character, like "powerful," "hungry," "dreamy," etc. Then write a list of activities, like "reading the newspaper" and "eating dinner." Get your sidekick to do the same, then cut the words out, fold them up, and separate the feelings and activities into two bowls. Take turns to draw a slip from each bowl and silently perform the action given in the style given. The other person must guess both words/phrases from body language alone.

 Smoke signals: One of the most useful ways an understanding of body language can help is by revealing when someone is lying to you. Bear in mind, too, that defensive body language can indicate a person is keeping something from you.

Understand Body Language **Form**

Once you have mastered this **Way to Become a Superhero**, stick your Achieved Star here and fill in the form

Achieved

——————— DRAMATIC SILENCE ———————

1. Pick an episode of a drama series or soap opera to watch. It's important you choose one you know nothing about. You'll need to be able to pause and rewind the show, so record it first or watch it online.
2. With the SOUND TURNED OFF, watch the first four scenes, pausing after each one to make a note in the chart below of the body language clues you've picked up from the actors and what they tell you about the relationships between characters and what is happening or being discussed.
3. After the fourth scene, write your prediction about what will happen in the rest of the show in the space provided below.
4. Rewind to the start and watch the whole show with the sound turned up. How accurate were your guesses about the characters and plot? Go back to the chart and give yourself ratings out of ten. Did you correctly predict what would happen?

SCENE NO.	BODY LANGUAGE	RELATIONSHIPS	PLOT
1	___ /10	___ /10	___ /10
2	___ /10	___ /10	___ /10
3	___ /10	___ /10	___ /10
4	___ /10	___ /10	___ /10

What do you predict will happen in the rest of the show, based on what you've seen so far?

Did you use this power for...

GOOD? or **EVIL?**

Did you predict correctly? [y/n]

When you misunderstood what was going on, was this because . . .

. . . the body language was subtle? [y/n]   . . . the acting was terrible? [y/n]   . . . your skills were poor? [y/n]

At the same time you could master these other **Ways:**
12: Mind Control • **72**: Speak a Hundred Languages • **74**: Identify and Interpret Clues
89: Know When Someone's Lying • **92**: Telepathy • **93**: Develop Powers of Persuasion

Become a Science Genius

There's a special chemistry between science and superpowers. Both offer an almost godlike ability to create, to transform, and to destroy. So grab your lab coat and a guinea pig (your sidekick will do) and get experimenting.

Science Faction

- If you want to break the speed of light, travel through time, or replicate objects (or yourself), you'll need to study physics. Start with the basics, like making a rocket (see opposite for instructions). Then all you have to do is work out how to make one without a balloon.
- Study biology and be inspired by the survival tactics and ingenuity of the natural world. Spider-Man's powers and gadgets were modeled on arachnids' abilities. Choose an animal with skills you'd really like to have, and study how they manage to do the things they do. Design and build some equipment that might help you copy those skills.
- Chemistry will give you an understanding of the composition of all matter and how it interacts. You don't have to have a fancy laboratory when you begin your research; a kitchen will do, testing with substances like water, salt, vinegar, or sugar. For instance, if you were interested in developing supercool (as in freezing) powers, you could experiment with baking soda to make icicles (see opposite).
- Whatever experiments you conduct as part of your superhero research and development, be very careful and take all the necessary safety precautions. We all know what happens when science goes wrong.*

---

*When science goes wrong: Perhaps your aim is to become the next Dr. Octopus, in which case you'll happily dabble with radioactive substances or throw yourself into a vat of chemicals and come out smiling like the Joker—kiss your good looks good-bye, though.

Become a Science Genius **Form**

Once you have mastered this **Way to Become a Superhero**, stick your Achieved Star here and fill in the form

☆ **Achieved**

ROCKET SCIENCE

WHAT YOU NEED: a long piece of string • a drinking straw • a long balloon • clothespin • adhesive tape

WHAT TO DO: Tie one end of the string to a sturdy support (e.g., a chair, table leg, or tree) and thread the other end through the straw. Pull the string taut and tie the loose end to another support at the same height so the track is level.

Blow up your balloon as big as possible without bursting it, but don't tie a knot at the end—use a clothespin instead. If that doesn't work, just trap the valve between your fingers.

Tape the balloon to the straw, as shown, and pull it back to the start of the track so that the nose of the balloon faces toward the far end of the string. It's time to release the air . . .

How long was your string track? `0 . 0` ft

Did the balloon travel the whole length? `y/n`

What is the name of the force that propels the rocket forward? Unscramble the letters.

HURTST

☐☐☐☐☐☐

See if you can modify the balloon rocket to make it travel farther. Did you succeed? `y/n`

If yes, what did you change?

The length/type of straw `y/n`   The shape/size of the balloon `y/n`

The length/type of string `y/n`   The level/angle of the track `y/n`

Describe what you did

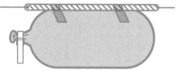

CRYSTAL ICE

WHAT YOU NEED: two glasses • warm water • baking soda • two paper clips • string • a saucer

WHAT TO DO: Fill the glasses two-thirds full with warm water and stir baking soda into them until no more will dissolve. Tie a paper clip to either end of the string and drop them into the two glasses, so that the string is suspended between them, as shown.

Place a saucer under the string and leave it to stand for a few days. As the string soaks up the solution, an icicle should begin to grow down from it.

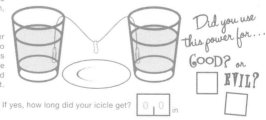

Did you use this power for . . . **GOOD?** or ☐ **EVIL?** ☐

Did your experiment work? `y/n` If yes, how long did your icicle get? `0 . 0` in

At the same time you could master these other **Ways**:
3: Take Flight • **29:** Solve Impossible Problems • **55:** Break Codes • **64:** Travel in Time • **77:** X-Ray Vision • **79:** Design Your Own Gadgets • **94:** Talk to Computers

Strike a Superhero Pose

Being a superhero isn't just about doing good, but looking good too. When that lucky photographer manages to snap a rare picture of you, it will be blazoned across all the front pages, so you want to be sure you're giving the right impression. Think of yourself as an icon—what do you represent? Your pose needs to tell people what you're all about, inspire them with awe, and make your enemies quake in their dirty little boots.

Come On, Vogue

- What is your single most super superpower? Do you want to convey physical skills or mental ones? And what about your character? Are you bold and brassy or dark and soulful? Your pose has to sum up all these things—with the help of your costume and name, of course. It must belong to you and only you.
- This isn't the time to flaunt your acting skills—just because you can swim like a fish doesn't mean you should blow bubbles and do the breaststroke. If you're fast, you don't have to do a running pose—imagine you're speed itself. You want to inspire confidence, not make people laugh. Try to combine power with a degree of elegance.
- What's your best feature? Obviously you want to show it off to its best advantage. If you have mesmeric eyes, perhaps you can do something with your arms and hands to draw attention to them. Don't be coy. You don't have to have the perfect body—even a big belly can become a deadly weapon. The most important thing is that you look confident.

Face-off: You've got your power stance, your arms and legs are in position—now don't forget your face. There's no point posing like a superbrained scientist or a kung-fu master if your expression's that of a knucklehead. Eyebrow-arching is always a good idea . . .

Strike a Superhero Pose **Form**

Once you have mastered this **Way to Become a Superhero**, stick your Achieved Star here and fill in the form

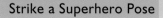

Achieved

SUPERPOSER

Try out a few different poses. Take a photograph of you in your outfit and place the best poses in the spaces below. Stick your final favorite pose in the frame in the middle of the page.

Place a photo or draw your superhero pose here

Name of pose here

Place a photo or draw your superhero pose here

Name of pose here

Place a photo or draw your superhero pose here

Name of pose here

Place a photo or draw your superhero pose here

Name of pose here

Place a photo of your favorite superhero pose here

Name of pose here

Place a photo or draw your superhero pose here

Name of pose here

What is your best feature?

Ask your sidekick to assess your pose and give you three words that come to mind

Did you use this power for... **GOOD?** or **EVIL?**

☐

What is your top superpower?

☐

Does your pose show these off? [y/n]

Have you achieved your desired effect? [y/n]

If not, keep working at it!

At the same time you could master these other **Ways**:
1: Discover Your Alter Ego • **2**: Choose Your Name • **9**: Select a Sidekick
17: Choose Your Outfit • **28**: Balance • **46**: Choose a Cause • **99**: Gather a Superteam

Invisibility

Scientists have been working on invisibility cloaks for years, but until this technology is available, you'll have to employ more self-reliant methods. Invisibility gives you a huge tactical advantage, enabling you to spy on your enemy or creep up and disarm them before they even know you're there.

Now You See Me, Now You Don't

- Being invisible isn't simply about making yourself disappear—poof! It's about making yourself hard to see and hard to hear, blending in with your surroundings so that you're utterly inconspicuous, which means even if you are seen, you aren't necessarily noticed. So the first thing to do is to assess your surroundings. How can you blend in?
- There are many ways to camouflage oneself. Clothing is an obvious one: as a rough guide, wear greens/browns in the country, dark blue/gray (not black) at night, and blue/gray for the city. Moving fluently and not making any sudden or unusual movements is another.
- Use the natural elements of your surroundings for cover. If they aren't big enough to completely conceal you, you need to blend in beside them. Shape your body like your cover. Look for obstacles and shadows you can use for cover as you sneak around. Practice running, crouching, rolling, and diving between natural covers.
- Practice moving around invisibly in different terrains. Find out where friends or family members are going to be and secretly go along too. Your mission is to shadow them for an hour without being spotted.

The scientific method: The most promising invisibility-cloak technology being developed uses clever "metamaterials" that bend light waves around them as they reflect off the surface (like water flowing over a stone), fooling the eye into believing nothing is there.

Invisibility Form

Once you have mastered this **Way to Become a Superhero**, stick your Achieved Star here and fill in the form

Achieved

--- **HAPPY STALK** ---

Put your powers of invisibility to the test as you secretly, and stealthily, tail your sidekick. On the map below, record the time and location when you started and finished tailing them. Also mark on the route any notable landmarks or places where your sidekick stopped.

Why did you stop tailing your sidekick?

☐ I was spotted   ☐ I had other things to do

☐ I lost them   ☐ They reached their destination

Start location

Time :

End location

Time :

How long did you tail them for?

0 0 hours   0 0 mins   0 0 secs

Were you on foot all the way? ☐ y/n

If no, what other forms of transport did you use?

☐ Bike   ☐ Bus   ☐ Car   ☐ Train   ☐ Plane   ☐ Boat

Other (please specify)
☐

Was your sidekick acting suspiciously? ☐ y/n

If yes, what was he/she up to?

Did people notice you acting suspiciously? ☐ y/n

If yes, did this cause problems? ☐ y/n

What elements in your surroundings did you use for cover?

☐ Trees   ☐ Bushes   ☐ People   ☐ Doorways   ☐ Dumpsters   ☐ Walls

Other (please specify)

What were you wearing? Draw your camouflage outfit below:

Rate your powers of invisibility

☆ Terrible   ☆ Poor

☆ Okay   ☆ Very good

☆ Excellent   ☆ Super-human

Did you use this power for... GOOD? ☐ or EVIL? ☐

At the same time you could master these other **Ways**:
10: Stealth • **17**: Choose Your Outfit • **28**: Balance • **39**: Speed • **47**: Master of Illusion • **60**: Save the World from the Undead • **66**: Agility • **85**: Shape-Shift

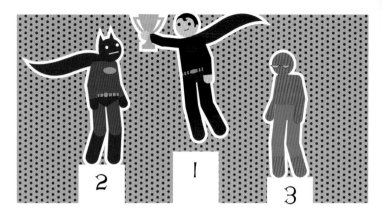

Never Give Up

When your nemesis turns to you and says, "Hey, Blob Boy" (or whatever name you go by), "you'll never get me!" you can't shrug your shoulders and say, "Okay, I'll be heading home then." You have to believe you can and you will get them, and promise them that whenever they turn around, you'll be there.

Stay on Target

- Have you ever walked away from a task or a game because you decided you were doomed to failure and couldn't see the point? Try to remember three occasions when you were—go on, admit it—a big loser. How can you make amends? Now go back and face those challenges.
- Routinely test your willpower by giving up any small bad habits, like biting your nails or not putting your clothes away. You can also practice by doing something that's useful or good for you but really quite boring every day for a week, like exercising or cleaning or practicing scales or reciting the times tables up to 20.
- Is there something you've always wanted to be good at but lacked the talent for? It's time to dedicate mind, body, and soul to the study of that subject or skill, and show what can be done with a supersteely power of will. Think positive, make a plan with clear goals (e.g., passing exams or completing a course), and stick to it. It will be worth the effort.
- Don't stop there. Enter competitions to be the best in your town, your state, your country—the world! It may take time, but don't give up until you have that Oscar/Nobel Prize/Grammy, etc., in your hands.

 In the words of Winston Churchill, "Never give in, never give in, never, never, never, never . . ." Sheer single-mindedness is something shared by superheroes and villains alike, which might explain why they often have such long-running feuds and vendettas.

Never Give Up **Form**

Once you have mastered this **Way to Become a Superhero**,
stick your Achieved Star here and fill in the form

Achieved

——————— WITHOUT FAIL ———————

Pick a subject or skill you're terrible at but would love to learn, and apply yourself to the task of
becoming world champion. Monitor your progress over 10 weeks using the graph below—but
don't give up until you hit the top line (you may have to change "weeks" to "years"!)

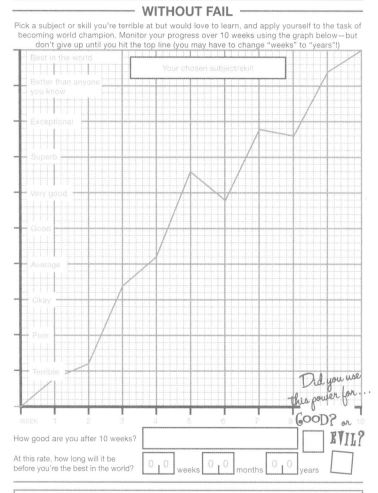

Your chosen subject/skill

Best in the world

Better than anyone
you know

Exceptional

Superb

Very good

Good

Average

Okay

Poor

Terrible

WEEK 1 2 3 4 5 6 7 8 9 10

Did you use this power for... **GOOD?** or **EVIL?**

How good are you after 10 weeks?

At this rate, how long will it be
before you're the best in the world?
0|0 weeks 0|0 months 0|0 years

At the same time you could master these other **Ways**:
6: Stamina • **13**: Conquer Your Fears • **26**: Know Your Weaknesses • **53**: Be Ruthless
70: Cope Under Pressure • **84**: Resist Temptation • **100**: Devise Your Villainous Comeback

Save the World from Scary Monsters

You never know when a huge dinosaur might rise, Godzilla-like, from the ocean, or somewhere in a lab a scientist might accidentally inject a spider with a growth hormone causing a new species of giant arachnids to evolve. The key is to be prepared for all eventualities.

All Creatures Great and Small

- Before tackling a monster, observe its methods of attack and defense and look for weaknesses. For example, if they're tentacled, their reach and multitasking capabilities will be particularly problematic. If they have one eye, taking this out would be a sensible first step in rendering your terrifying beast as harmless as a kitten. Big beasts are usually lumbering and slow, so you'll be able to combat this with your speed and agility.

- The ideal way to train for this kind of fight is to try to simulate it. Devise an outfit for your sidekick modeled on the monster's appearance and—as far as you can manage it—size. As you design away, be aware of any potential vulnerable points on the creature's body, and think about how you might best take advantage of them. Don't spend too long making the monster suit look convincing—you don't want to inflict injury on your ally by momentarily forgetting it isn't the real foe you're attacking. Also, ultimately, you're likely to destroy the suit, so you don't want hours of meticulous work to end up in a mash of cardboard and tentacles on the floor.

 Patter of tiny feet: Don't be fooled by size. Some of the deadliest monsters are also the smallest. From killer bees to gremlins, you're looking at creatures that rarely work alone. Watch out for their speed, stealth, razor-sharp teeth, or lethal poison and sheer numbers.

Save the World . . .
from Scary Monsters **Form**

Once you have mastered this **Way to Become a Superhero**, stick your Achieved Star here and fill in the form

Achieved

SCARY MONSTERS
KNOW YOUR ENEMY

Draw the most terrifying beast your imagination can conjure up and consider how you would take it on. If you're mentally, physically, and strategically prepared for the worst, you should be able to deal with whatever eventually comes your way.

Draw the creature of your worst nightmares below.

Your beast's strengths

Your beast's weaknesses

CONFIDENTIAL

YOU NEED A PLAN OF ACTION. WILL YOU . . .

. . . set up a trap and try to lure it in?   y/n

. . . focus on disabling its most dangerous weapon?   y/n

. . . attempt to tame it?   y/n

. . . find a way to poison it?   y/n

. . . call in the army for assistance?   y/n

. . . hope they kill each other in battle?   y/n

Explain how you will carry out your plan below.

Did you use this power for . . .
GOOD? or
☐ EVIL?
☐

At the same time you could master these other **Ways**:
13: Conquer Your Fears • **14**: Strength • **22**: Communicate with Animals • **33**. Anticipate Your Enemy's Next Move • **39**: Speed • **63**: Observation Skills • **73**: Create a Force Field

S.U.P.E.R.
Support for
Unique People
Exhibiting
Radioactivity

H.E.R.O.E.S.
Help for
Expired & Retired,
Outstanding &
Extraordinary
Superheroes

P.O.W.E.R.
Protection
Of Worldwide
Evil Rulers

Choose a Cause

The great war of good against evil can be fought on many fronts. It is a brave but rather naive superhero who thinks he or she can defeat evil in every form wherever it may reside. Don't bite off more than you can chew, because you will end up doing many things but none of them terribly well. There are plenty of criminal masterminds out there if you only turn over the right stones. So learn to share the burden with your superhero colleagues.

Rebel with a Cause

- Look at your specialist skills (assuming you have some!) to decide what sort of enemy you are best equipped to deal with. What are your key areas of knowledge? For example, if math is your strong point, perhaps you should specialize in criminals operating in the world of finance.
- What issues do you feel most strongly about? You're looking for a cause you can feel passionate about, but not one you will lose your head over. Personal vendettas are a dangerous business. If revenge is your primary motivation, just remember: it is a dish best served cold.
- Once you've made your decision, compose a motto and clearly state your aims so there can be no confusion as to the just nature of your cause. For example, if you have chosen to save the world from aliens, your motto might be: "Don't talk to strangers, especially green ones," or "Cleaning up America's skies," or "One head good, three heads bad."
- Make sure others know what your cause is so they know to contact you when evil is going down on your watch.

Uncommon goal: Steer clear of causes that are too specialist, like ridding the world of six-toed, cross-eyed Moldovan evil geniuses, or lost causes, such as the right to life for dodos. You could find work in rather short supply or else a total waste of time.

Choose a Cause **Form**

Once you have mastered this **Way to Become a Superhero**,
stick your Achieved Star here and fill in the form

Achieved

CAUSE AND EFFECT

A manifesto is a public declaration of an organization or political party's aims, objectives,
and motives. As you begin to define your campaign for good (or evil), you too should have a
manifesto, so that everyone (yourself included) can be sure about what you stand for.

(Your supername here)'S MANIFESTO

DECLARATION: I have a vision for the world in which
peace & order/anarchy & chaos/I* reign. (*delete as appropriate)

My campaign will concentrate on the following areas:

Oppression ☐   Corruption ☐

Environmental disaster ☐   War ☐

General human suffering ☐   Crime ☐

Other (please specify)

_____

My primary objectives are:

_____
_____
_____
_____

These objectives can be achieved with the following resources/skills at my disposal:

_____
_____
_____
_____

The campaign's driving force is my . . .

. . . respect for humankind ☐   . . . scorn for humankind ☐

. . . desire for justice ☐   . . . desire for power/money ☐

. . . need for revenge ☐   . . . insanity ☐

Other (please specify)

_____

CAMPAIGN MOTTO:

Was this cause used for . . .

GOOD? or

☐ **EVIL?**

☐

At the same time you could master these other **Ways**:
30: Save the World from Alien Attack • **31**: Identify Your Nemesis
49: Hone Your Moral Compass • **75**: Save the World from Environmental Disaster

Master of Illusion

If you can make someone believe something is real when it's not, you can influence their behavior—as long as the deception isn't discovered (or, at least, not until it's too late). For example, if you can convince your enemy you have him surrounded, he may give himself up without a fight.

Making a False Impression

- Some illusions are all about sleight of hand, like making small objects vanish and reappear. Start by learning how to palm a coin and do the French drop (you'll find lots of tutorials on the Internet), and practice in front of a mirror. Perfect the technique before showing anyone.
- Houdini could make an elephant vanish. Clearly this illusion wasn't merely a case of sleight of hand. Often the illusionist needs specially designed props. See if you can design a prop that will make something disappear or seemingly transform into something else. An object like this could be handy for stashing your most important and secret objects.
- Grand-scale illusions require careful planning and rehearsal—always practice with small models first. For example, you could try making an object or figure appear like a ghost out of thin air using a sheet of Plexiglas, a black cloth, and a flashlight (see opposite). This "Pepper's ghost" illusion has been used to scare people in theaters since the 19th century.
- Not all illusions are optical. Learning to throw your voice can give the illusion of being somewhere you're not, and being able to accurately imitate sounds can give the illusion that you're something you're not.

 Tactical magic: Governments have employed illusionists in times of trouble. The British magician Maskelyne devised ways to disguise tanks, factories, and cities during the Second World War, and Robert-Houdin subdued rebellious natives in the French colony of Algeria with his magic displays.

Master of Illusion **Form**

Once you have mastered this **Way to Become a Superhero**, stick your Achieved Star here and fill in the form

Achieved

PEPPER'S GHOST

WHAT YOU NEED: a black cloth • an object to project (light-colored objects work best, since they reflect more light) • a sheet of Plexiglas • a flashlight

WHAT TO DO:

1. Use your black cloth to create a backdrop for your object to sit in front of (you may need to attach it to a wall or drape it over a pile of books). Position your object against the black background and make sure it is sitting on black cloth too.

2. Place the sheet of Plexiglas some distance in front of the object in the spot where you would like your ghostly apparition to appear.

3. Turn the lights off and shine your flashlight directly onto the object. Does its reflection appear on the Plexiglas? You may need to adjust the position of the Plexiglas until the reflection is where you want it.

4. Find the best place to view the illusion, where the reflection of the object is clearly visible but the

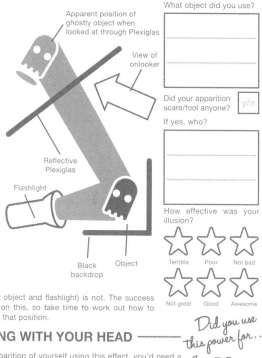

Apparent position of ghostly object when looked at through Plexiglas

View of onlooker

Reflective Plexiglas

Flashlight

Black backdrop

Object

Plexiglas sheet (and your object and flashlight) is not. The success of your illusion depends on this, so take time to work out how to maneuver your victim into that position.

What object did you use?

Did your apparition scare/fool anyone? `y/n`

If yes, who?

How effective was your illusion?

⭐ ⭐ ⭐
Terrible Poor Not bad

⭐ ⭐ ⭐
Not great Good Awesome

MESSING WITH YOUR HEAD

To produce a life-size apparition of yourself using this effect, you'd need a huge sheet of Plexiglas. But you could still scare your enemies with your ghostly appearance. You just need to use your head in place of the object above—quite literally. A disembodied floating head will be enough to give most tough guys the heebie-jeebies. Whiten your face with some makeup for the full effect—and be sure the rest of your body is dressed in black so it doesn't reflect in the Plexiglas too.

Did you use this power for...
GOOD? or
☐ **EVIL?**
☐

At the same time you could master these other **Ways**:
20: Learn to Multitask • 21: Dexterity • 29: Solve Impossible Problems
36: Be in Two Places at Once • 43: Invisibility • 52: Telekinesis • 85: Shape-Shift

Choose a Calling Card

What's the point of your careful planning and inventive showmanship if no one knows who's responsible for your brilliantly wicked deeds? Sometimes doing bad is its own reward (aside from the power and material gains), but a bit of respect would be nice too.

The Greatest Youdunnit

- The way to ensure this is to leave something at the crime scene that acts as your signature, that says you are the artist behind the dazzling work of chaos, like a playing card or an origami creature. Is there any aspect of your supervillain identity that suggests an apt calling card? For example, if you're a dashing black-hearted romantic villain, you might leave a black-painted rose with some nasty thorns on its stem.
- Think theatrically. You don't just have to leave physical objects. You could have a theme song that you leave playing on a portable sound device at the scene, or a symbol that you reflect into the air.
- If you're the intellectual type, why not leave a more cryptic clue, like a book with a title that hints at how you carried out your crime, or one that just has a good laugh in the face of the cops? If you kidnap someone, for example, you could leave a copy of *The Lady Vanishes*.
- Remember not to leave fingerprints or any traces of DNA on your calling card. Though you want people to know you're the culprit, you don't want them to find out your real identity, or it could be curtains for your career in crime.

Beware of copycat criminals: They might use your calling card to put the police off their scent. You don't want to get blamed for someone else's shoddy work. Make your calling card very particular so that detectives with any intelligence can tell the real from the fake.

Choose a Calling Card **Form**

Once you have mastered this **Way to Become an Evil Genius**, stick your Achieved Star here and fill in the form

Achieved

—————————— **GIVE US A CLUE . . .** ——————————

You probably have such a huge ego you won't be able to resist letting your do-good enemies know whodunit. Take a look at the ideas below and think which particular items you would leave as your calling cards.

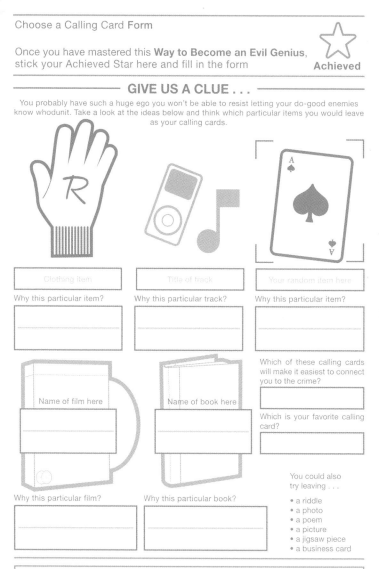

Clothing item

Why this particular item?

Title of track

Why this particular track?

Your random item here

Why this particular item?

Name of film here

Name of book here

Which of these calling cards will make it easiest to connect you to the crime?

Which is your favorite calling card?

Why this particular film?

Why this particular book?

You could also try leaving . . .

- a riddle
- a photo
- a poem
- a picture
- a jigsaw piece
- a business card

At the same time you could master these other **Ways**:
2: Choose Your Name • **7**: Decipher Devious Riddles • **11**: Groom Your Dark Side
23: Plan for World Domination • **59**: Take Risks

Hone Your Moral Compass

Life isn't all black and white: it's full of gray areas. So if you think you already know right from wrong, think again. If you're to fight for truth and justice, you need to define truth and justice and what is meant by "fight." How far will you go? How do you prioritize? To really hone your moral judgment you must be able to reason objectively. That isn't easy.

Wrong + Wrong = Not Right

- Listen to your conscience: it's your innate moral compass. You'd have to have grown up in a moral vacuum not to feel an atom of guilt when you do something to hurt somebody. Always think through the consequences of your and others' actions, both direct and indirect.
- Empathize. Before passing judgment on someone, make sure you've made an effort to understand why they behaved as they did.
- Try to understand a range of moral viewpoints. Read important religious and philosophical texts, and try to pull out the universally acknowledged moral statements.
- Familiarize yourself with the law so you know the legal definition of "wrong." It is a massively complex beast, so concentrate on the basics— you don't really need to know the minor details of every single bit of legislation. Learn some laws about common low-level crimes, and test your moral radar by seeing how many of these misdemeanors you can spot being committed in one day. Of course, once you're a fully qualified superhero, you won't need to bother with the small fry.

 Serve them all right: As a superhero, you have to do right by everyone, even your enemies. Don't let them goad you into a blind rage, making you lash out at them. You're not here to convert or to mete out punishments but to stop bad things from happening.

Hone Your Moral Compass **Form**

Once you have mastered this **Way to Become a Superhero**,
stick your Achieved Star here and fill in the form

Achieved

MORALLY WRONG

People break the law right under your nose every day. From littering to cycling on
the sidewalk, they may not all be life-threatening acts, but they're still criminal offenses.
Brush up on the law and see how many incidents you can spot in a day.

	DATE AND TIME OF INCIDENT	BRIEF DESCRIPTION OF CRIME AND PERPETRATOR	ACTION YOU TOOK, IF ANY
INCIDENT 1	: AM / PM m m d d y y		
INCIDENT 2	: AM / PM m m d d y y		
INCIDENT 3	: AM / PM m m d d y y		
INCIDENT 4	: AM / PM m m d d y y		
INCIDENT 5	: AM / PM m m d d y y		
INCIDENT 6	: AM / PM m m d d y y		

At the same time you could master these other **Ways**:
8: Kick Ass Humanely • **40**: Understand Body Language • **81**: Make the Right
Decisions—Fast • **88**: Acquire Specialist Knowledge • **89**: Know When Someone's Lying

Second Sight

Along with telepathy, seeing into the future is one of the extrasensory powers that can prove a curse as well as a blessing, as you may see things you don't want to see. But you just have to remember that the future is not set in stone. You're in control of your own destiny, and as a superhero of the future, you'll be gifted with powers that could alter the destiny of others.

As Far As I Can See . . .

- If you've ever had that déjà vu feeling, there's a good chance you're recalling some information from your subconscious, perhaps a vision of the future that you are now experiencing, and it may have roots in the locked memory of a dream. Premonitions have a history of coming to the "seer" in a dream, so start keeping a dream diary. To recall your dreams, tell yourself as you go to sleep that you want to wake up fully from a dream and remember it. This will act as an alarm clock. Or you can actually use an alarm clock, setting it to go off at 90-minute intervals when you are likely to be experiencing REM (dreaming) sleep. When you wake, hold your position and instantly try to cling on to what you were experiencing. Don't let other everyday worries distract you.
- On separate pieces of paper, write down some predictions for different times in the future—tomorrow, next week, next month, six months' time, and so on, up to five years in the future. Predict an event in your personal life as well as more global happenings. Put them in sealed envelopes only to be opened when the appointed time arrives.

Prophet of doom: Nostradamus was rather fond of predicting disasters like plague, drought, war, and floods, which is a pretty useful superhero skill to have. Some even credit him with foreseeing events like the Great Fire of London and the rise of Napoleon and Hitler.

Second Sight **Form**

Once you have mastered this **Way to Become a Superhero**,
stick your Achieved Star here and fill in the form

Achieved

THE FUTURE, TODAY . . .

Making predictions is easy—getting them right is the hard part. You're not just speculating about what
might happen—you want to receive a clear vision of the future. This requires concentrated meditation.
Close your eyes and see what the future holds. Record your predictions and their accuracy.

TOMORROW

m m d d y y at : I predict . . .

Rate the accuracy of your prediction
out of 5 (0 = way off, 5 = spot on)   5

What part, if any, did you get right?

NEXT WEEK

m m d d y y at : I predict . . .

Rate the accuracy of your prediction
out of 5 (0 = way off, 5 = spot on)   5

What part, if any, did you get right?

NEXT MONTH

m m d d y y at : I predict . . .

Rate the accuracy of your prediction
out of 5 (0 = way off, 5 = spot on)   5

What part, if any, did you get right?

NEXT YEAR

m m d d y y at : I predict . . .

Rate the accuracy of your prediction
out of 5 (0 = way off, 5 = spot on)   5

What part, if any, did you get right?

DREAM ON

Keep a dream diary for a week. Did you have any premonitions? If yes, what
event(s) do you think you might have foreseen? Write them in the box.

*Did you use
this power for . . .*

GOOD? or

☐ **EVIL?**

☐

Has your dream come true
yet?   y/n   Rate your second sight skills
(out of 10)   10

At the same time you could master these other **Ways**:
5: Super-Vision • **19**: Know Whom to Save First • **33**: Anticipate Your Enemy's Next Move
64: Travel in Time • **75**: Save the World from Environmental Disaster • **92**: Telepathy

Jump High

You weren't born with the legs of a flea, but that's the kind of champion level of jumping you should be aiming for. Imagine being able to pole-vault without the pole or pogo without the stick. Jumping isn't all about height either. You may have to leap across rooftops, so distance is important too. And, as with most physical challenges, courage is paramount. Faced with a vast abyss, you have to have the heart to make that leap of faith.

One Giant Leap for Mankind

- To make really big jumps, the key is in the speed of your running start. The faster you go, the more power you'll have in your spring as you launch. Use your arms to propel yourself up and through the air and always bend your knees as you land.
- Doing the high jump, long jump, and hurdles at school or an athletics club will help you measure your efforts against mere mortals'. You can also practice at home, jumping on the spot (you might not always get a running start) or over obstacles (like a chair), jumping distances (like from the TV to the sofa), and jumping backward and sideways (important evasive moves).
- Build up leg strength by jumping repeatedly on and off a step. Though they're only small jumps, each one will give the muscles you need a workout. Don't forget to include some stretches in your exercise routine to improve flexibility. Have more fun while you practice jumping by playing games like basketball and volleyball.

 Perfect landings: If you're leaping at speed, diving into a roll as you land will help keep up forward momentum and lessen the impact of your landing. Rolling on to your shoulder or back also helps to break a fall when you're jumping off something high.

Jump High **Form**

Once you have mastered this **Way to Become a Superhero**,
stick your Achieved Star here and fill in the form

Achieved

——— YET ANOTHER HURDLE ———

Running is all well and good, but without the ability to jump high and far, a superhero would fall at
the first fence. Try these jumping tests.

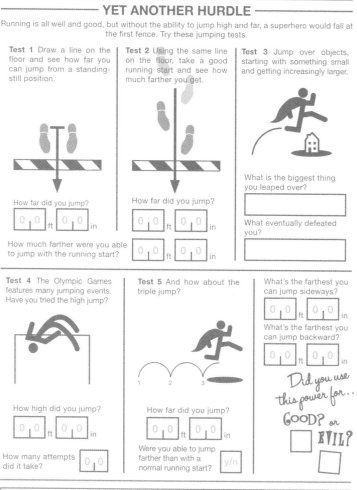

Test 1 Draw a line on the floor and see how far you can jump from a standing-still position.

How far did you jump?

| 0 | 0 | ft | 0 | 0 | in |

How much farther were you able to jump with the running start?

Test 2 Using the same line on the floor, take a good running start and see how much farther you get.

How far did you jump?

| 0 | 0 | ft | 0 | 0 | in |

| 0 | 0 | ft | 0 | 0 | in |

Test 3 Jump over objects, starting with something small and getting increasingly larger.

What is the biggest thing you leaped over?

What eventually defeated you?

Test 4 The Olympic Games features many jumping events. Have you tried the high jump?

How high did you jump?

| 0 | 0 | ft | 0 | 0 | in |

How many attempts did it take? | 0 | 0 |

Test 5 And how about the triple jump?

1   2   3

How far did you jump?

| 0 | 0 | ft | 0 | 0 | in |

Were you able to jump farther than with a normal running start? | y/n |

What's the farthest you can jump sideways?

| 0 | 0 | ft | 0 | 0 | in |

What's the farthest you can jump backward?

| 0 | 0 | ft | 0 | 0 | in |

Did you use this power for…

GOOD? *or*

| | **EVIL?**

| |

At the same time you could master these other **Ways**:

3: Take Flight • **13**: Conquer Your Fears • **14**: Strength • **28**: Balance • **66**: Agility

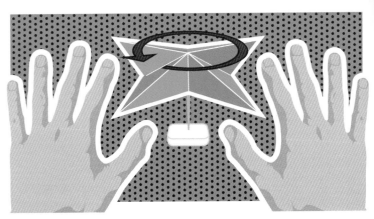

Telekinesis

Sometimes you just can't get to that weapon/switch/chocolate bar, etc., fast enough. Perhaps you can't get there at all because your hands are tied up with fighting off deadly ninjas or the whole of you is tied up, tightly, with ropes. It would be handy to move things with the power of thought alone.

Moving the Goalposts

- You need to become one with the object you want to control, to free your mind of any distractions that may prevent you from tuning in to every atom of it. To test your concentration, draw a black dot on a piece of paper and see how long you can focus on it without words or other images entering your mind. Every time your brain strays, write down how long you lasted. You should aim for five minutes of unbroken focus. Then do this exercise with an object. Start at the top and slowly take in every part of it until you know it so well you can virtually feel it!
- Now try moving something. The lighter the object the better, so there's less resistance to the energy of your mind. Try a smooth round pencil, a piece of paper or a psi wheel (see opposite). Moving your hands may help you channel your thought waves toward it more effectively, but when you get really good, this won't be necessary. Try bending spoons and levitating objects too—it all works on the same principle.
- No luck? Well, you could always cheat. Invest in some invisible thread or a small, powerful magnet and experiment with what you can appear to achieve without touching objects directly with your hands.

 Spooked out: Suffering from poltergeists? Perhaps what you're really experiencing are your hidden telekinetic powers struggling to find expression. This theory is held by many, who point to troubled adolescents around whom poltergeist activity often seems to center.

Telekinesis **Form**

Once you have mastered this **Way to Become a Superhero**, stick your Achieved Star here and fill in the form

☆ **Achieved**

SPIN ON THIS

Begin your journey into the world of telekinesis with this simple experiment. You should be able to achieve instant results with a homemade psi wheel.

Things you'll need:
A small square piece of paper (such as a Post-it note)

An eraser

A needle

1. Fold the square diagonally one way . . .

2. Open the square out and fold it diagonally the other way . . .

3. When you open it out again your square should look like this. >

< 4. Turn the square over, then fold it vertically.

> 5. Open the square out and fold it horizontally.

6. Now your square should look like this. >

7. Pinch the square to make it look like a four-pointed star.

8. Take the needle and stick it in the eraser. Make sure the needle is standing perfectly vertical. Then balance the paper on top as shown.

9. Now concentrate your thoughts on the psi wheel and place your hands on either side of the paper . . .

Did you make it spin? y/n

Left?

Right?

If the psi wheel turned, what do you think caused this?

Your mind

Science

Explain your conclusion in the box below . . .

The psi wheel turned because . . .

Did you use this power for . . .

GOOD? or

EVIL?

At the same time you could master these other **Ways**:
12: Mind Control • **20**: Learn to Multitask • **36**: Be in Two Places at Once
69: Kung-Fu Master • **73**: Create a Force Field • **92**: Telepathy • **94**: Talk to Computers

Be Ruthless

In the world of big bad bullies there is no room for sentimentality or trying to see things from other people's points of view. You have to be single-minded and utterly selfish. No one will like you for this, but that's the point. If you are essentially a nice person, and acting in this really mean way is not something that comes naturally, then you need to follow the training program below.

Fears for Tears

- Get some friends together (if you have any) and hold a movie night. Recommended viewing would be any of the following: *Bambi*, *Ghost*, *ET*, *It's a Wonderful Life*, *Titanic*, *Old Yeller*, and *Marley and Me*. These are all well-known tearjerkers, and if you really want to put your callousness to the test, you'll sit through any of these movies and allow yourself to be monitored for wet eyes, sniffling, or out-and-out sobbing. Complete the list without shedding a tear and you get full points. Bonus points are available if you laugh at the saddest parts.
- When was the last time you cleaned your room? Even if you're obsessively tidy, to prove your ruthlessness you should put yourself through the clear-out of your life. Every scrap of paper, cuddly toy, photograph, and e-mail must be assessed for sentimental value and ditched if found to have no purpose other than to give you a warm feeling. If you're going to make excuses for keeping such useless items, then perhaps evil genius isn't the career for you.

Sob stories: Films aren't the only way to test your cold-heartedness. Try to get through these books with dry eyes: *The Happy Prince*, *Charlotte's Web*, *The Book Thief*, *Tess of the D'Urbervilles*, *One Flew Over the Cuckoo's Nest*, and *Danny the Champion of the World*.

Be Ruthless **Form**

Once you have mastered this **Way to Become an Evil Genius**, stick your Achieved Star here and fill in the form

Achieved

——— YOU SENTIMENTAL FOOL ———

Rid yourself of those possessions that serve no purpose other than to give you that faraway look in your eye as you recall some happy memory. Oh . . . okay, then. If you must you can simply lock them away in a box instead. But only bring them out when you're sure you're alone!

OLD TOYS

How many did you get rid of?

`0 , 0 , 0`

Which one was hardest to ditch?

Did you . . .

. . . chuck it? ☐   . . . destroy it? ☐

. . . give it away? ☐   . . . put it in the attic? ☐

Which ones, if any, did you save?

TEXT MESSAGES

How many did you get rid of?

`0 , 0 , 0`

Which one was hardest to ditch?

Who was it from?

Did you sneakily write it down before deleting it?   `y/n`

Which ones, if any, did you save?

PHOTOS

How many did you get rid of?

`0 , 0 , 0`

Which one was hardest to ditch?

Who/what was it of?

Did you erase the file and any hard copies?   `y/n`

Which ones, if any, did you save?

SOUVENIRS

How many did you get rid of?

`0 , 0 , 0`

Which one was hardest to ditch?

Why was it so special?

Which ones, if any, did you save?

WHAT ELSE WILL YOU CHUCK IN YOUR CLEAR-OUT?

List the items below . . .

As you threw these items out, were you . . .

. . . crying hysterically? ☐

. . . fighting back tears? ☐

. . . emotionless? ☐

. . . laughing hysterically? ☐

Do you feel better after your clear-out? `y/n`

At the same time you could master these other **Ways**:
11: Groom Your Dark Side • **23**: Plan for World Domination • **37**: Train Your Superpet
44: Never Give Up • **46**: Choose a Cause • **82**: Get a Head for Business

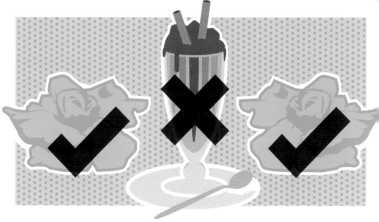

Make Sacrifices

During your superhero career you'll be faced with many hard decisions, often having to choose between something you love and the Right Thing to Do. And if you've nailed this superhero thing, you know already that the loser will usually turn out to be you. While your friends are at a rock concert or a party, you may be called away to clean the streets of crime. The best way to steel yourself for the sacrificial challenges that lie ahead is to get used to turning down the things you love, even when they're offered to you on a plate.

Special Offer!

- Ask your sidekick to prepare a dish of your favorite food—for example, a delicious chocolate cake. Also ask them to prepare something nutritious but utterly unappealing, like a plate of Brussels sprouts. Presented with both, you must choose superheroically. If you do the Right Thing, you must then watch your sidekick dig into the chocolate cake you honorably turned down. Remind yourself of the reasons you're doing it as you chomp down on that green bilge.
- Making the right decision is one thing, sticking to it is another. Decide that you're going to live without something you love for a week, or a month, or, if you're really tough, a whole year. Let someone who knows you really well decide what that thing should be and let them help you monitor your progress. You can put the time or money released by your abstinence toward your superhero efforts.

 Letting go: To truly appreciate the value of human life, superheroes must free themselves of any attachment to material goods. They must conquer selfish feelings to see the bigger picture. Next time someone says, "I love your watch," take it off and give it to them.

Make Sacrifices **Form**

Once you have mastered this **Way to Become a Superhero**, stick your Achieved Star here and fill in the form

Achieved

GIVE IT UP

On average, how many hours a week do you spend . . .

. . . watching TV? | 0 , 0 | . . . surfing the Internet? | 0 , 0 | . . . on the phone? | 0 , 0 | . . . on computer games? | 0 , 0 |

Which one do you do the most?

Test your ability to make sacrifices by giving up this activity for a week. Spend the hours you've saved helping other people instead.

What did you do with the hours you saved?

Who did it benefit?

Did you last the whole week?

y/n If not, how many hours did you lose to your old habit? | 0 , 0 |

How hard was it to make this sacrifice?

| | No problem | | Easy | | Very easy |
| | Hard | | Very hard | | Impossible |

Rate the following naughty-but-nice foods . . .

Chips | out of 10 | Candy | out of 10 | Cookies | out of 10 | Cake | out of 10 | Fast food | out of 10 | Chocolate | out of 10 |

Which one is your favorite?

Test your ability to make sacrifices by giving up this food for a week, replacing it with something healthy and nutritious instead.

What did you eat instead?

Do you feel much healthier now? | y/n |

Did you last the whole week? | y/n |

If not, how many times did you give in to your bad food habit? | 0 , 0 , 0 |

How hard was it to make this sacrifice?

| | No problem | | Easy | | Very easy |
| | Hard | | Very hard | | Impossible |

How much money do you get a month? | $ 0 , 0 . 0 , 0 |

What do you plan to do with this month's money?

Test your ability to make sacrifices by giving some of your allowance to charity this month.
How much did you give up?

| | None | | 1/4 | | 1/2 | | All |

Which charity did you give it to?

How hard was it to make this sacrifice?

| | No problem | | Easy | | Very easy |
| | Hard | | Very hard | | Impossible |

If you're serious about being a superhero, you should consider giving some of your allowance to charity every month.
Do you feel ready to do this? | y/n |

At the same time you could master these other **Ways**:
13: Conquer Your Fears • **26**: Know Your Weaknesses • **78**: Be a Good Influence
81: Make the Right Decisions—Fast • **84**: Resist Temptation • **86**: Keep Supersecrets

Break Codes

Evil geniuses aren't stupid. They won't make it easy for you to stumble across their secret plans. If they have any sense, they will code their communications to their minions. What they won't plan on is your ability to intercept and break these codes. Stay one step ahead of the enemy.

Inspector Morse

- The first thing to do when analyzing coded writing is to count up how often each symbol in the code is used. There's a good chance that one of the most frequently used ones represents the letter "e." What are the other most common letters in English? It helps to know these things.
- Look at one-, two-, or three-letter words. These will be the quickest to break because there are fewer options. There are only two words with one letter: "a" and "I," so if you've got one of these in your code, you get a head start. Once you've got "a," finding "n" and "d" should be easier, as "and" is such a common word too.
- Study words with double letters in them. It's fairly safe to assume that where you get a four-letter coded word with two identical symbols in the middle, that symbol will represent a vowel, of which only two are generally repeated: "o" and "e." If you suspect a double letter of being a consonant, you can cross quite a few candidates off the list, like "w," "h," "j," and "q."
- There's a message in code for you to solve on the opposite page, so get practicing. And remember—a good code-breaker is a good code-maker. See if you can create your own uncrackable codes.

Idiots: If you intercept a bizarre message from a villain, be on your guard. They could be using an indecipherable "idiot code." For example, "toilet paper" could be a command signal for "attack." So **"Go to Washington and get me toilet paper"** could mean **"Attack Washington now!"**

Break Codes **Form**

Once you have mastered this **Way to Become a Superhero**, stick your Achieved Star here and fill in the form

Achieved

DECODE

See if you can break this code:

4-(10)-(7)-11-9-7 / (15)-(3)-6-15 / 9-11-13-2 / 4-15-6-(10)-3 / (15)-(3)-2 / 7-2-16 / 5-2-(7)-11-8

> Write your answer here

It's a tricky one. Have a look at the key to the code below, and see if you can work it out now.

```
  1           5           9          13
  A           B           C           D
2   3       6   7       10  11      14  15
EF   GH     IJ   KL     MN   OP     QR   ST
  UV          W           X          YZ
  4           8          12          16
```

If you're still struggling, here's a clue: some letters have been allocated the same number to make things harder for code-breakers. The brackets around a number tell the message recipient to translate this as the second letter given to that number—without brackets the number refers to the first letter given. For example, "kill" would be written "7-6-(7)-(7)." Answers at the back of the book.

ENCODE

Now create your own code based on the model above. In the key to that code, the alphabet read left to right in three lines. Make your code even harder by mixing up the order and randomly allocating letters to numbers. Be careful not to allocate a letter to more than one number though. When you've finished, write a secret coded message to your sidekick and see how quickly they can solve it using your key.

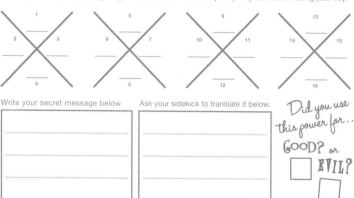

Write your secret message below.   Ask your sidekick to translate it below.

Did you use this power for... **GOOD?** or ☐ **EVIL?** ☐

At the same time you could master these other **Ways**:
7: Decipher Devious Riddles • **29**: Solve Impossible Problems • **72**: Speak a Hundred Languages • **74**: Identify and Interpret Clues • **94**: Talk to Computers

Invent Some Great One-Liners

Most superheroes are all about action, not talk, and rightly so. It won't do to be gabbing away about this and that when you should be focused on saving the world. However, evil geniuses love the sound of their own voice and will use words like knives to cut their enemies down to size. So whichever you're aiming to be, it is crucial to study the art of articulacy.

Eat My Words!

- When it comes to your nemesis, each of you will try to outdo the other in a war of wits. You'll need a couple of excellent put-downs to humiliate your enemy and make them lose their cool, but you'll also need to hone the ability to think on your feet and come back with some great retorts to the insults they're likely to throw at you. And don't forget to work on your "surprise" lines, which you use when you interrupt them to spoil their sadistic fun/world-saving efforts.

- If you're veering toward the dark side, you should add a killer line to your repertoire that you produce only when you're about to pull the plug on a victim. A fond farewell line (though only in a deeply sarcastic way) as you leave your enemies struggling helplessly to cope with the mayhem you've caused is also essential.

- If you're aiming at superhero, you're going to do a lot of good and receive a lot of praise from people. It's vital you know how to take a compliment. "It's all in the line of duty" is a solid favorite, but you should try to come up with something more original.

 Make love and war: It's hard to hold down a relationship when you lead a double life or you're a psychotic egomaniac. So work on a couple of lines that will have the object of your affection swooning in your arms. Show yourself to be a poet as well as a warrior.

Invent Some Great One-Liners **Form**

Once you have mastered this **Way to Become a Superhero**, stick your Achieved Star here and fill in the form

☆ **Achieved**

——— VERY PUNNY ———

Record your best one-liners for posterity—you never know, you might get the opportunity to use them again.

YOUR MOST EXCELLENT PUT-DOWN LINE

Who was the victim of your one-liner?

What was said in the buildup to your one-liner?

What was your witty reply? Write it in the speech bubble.

What was the response to your one-liner?

Silence ☐   Cheers ☐   Laughter ☐

Groans ☐   A witty retort ☐   Rage ☐

YOUR MOST EXCELLENT FAREWELL LINE

Who was the victim of your one-liner?

What was said in the buildup to your one-liner?

What was your witty reply? Write it in the speech bubble.

What was the response to your one-liner?

Silence ☐   Cheers ☐   Laughter ☐

Groans ☐   A witty retort ☐   Rage ☐

YOUR SURPRISE APPEARANCE LINE

Who was the victim of your one-liner?

What was said in the buildup to your one-liner?

What was your witty reply? Write it in the speech bubble.

What was the response to your one-liner?

Silence ☐   Cheers ☐   Laughter ☐

Groans ☐   A witty retort ☐   Rage ☐

Record some of your other most excellent insults in the speech bubbles below

Did you use this skill for...

GOOD? ☐ or **EVIL?** ☐

At the same time you could master these other **Ways**:
7: Decipher Devious Riddles • **11**: Groom Your Dark Side • **65**: Talk Your Way Out of Trouble • **93**: Develop Powers of Persuasion • **100**: Devise Your Villainous Comeback

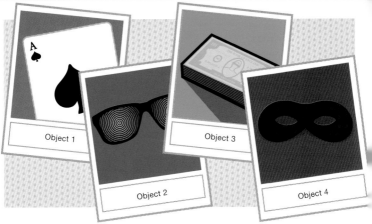

Object 1

Object 2

Object 3

Object 4

Photographic Memory

You could spend a lifetime learning everything that may be useful to you as guardian of the universe, but in the meantime that universe may be ravaged by an evil genius. So the first weapon you need in your intellectual arsenal is a mind that can recall everything it sees faster than—well, a speeding bullet.

I Came, I Saw, I Conquered

- We lose our natural ability to recall visual data in detail as we get older. Spend some time each day looking at a picture in a book, then close your eyes and try to visualize it in as much detail as possible. Do this exercise with words, numbers, and experiences too.
- Some people like to show off their amazing memories by reciting as many decimal places of pi as they can. Impressive but boring. You'd be better off training your memory by learning something a bit more useful, like words in a dictionary, or the numbers in a phone book, or the facts in *Guinness World Records*—that way you'll know how to contact the strongest, fastest, smallest, or tallest person when you need a bit of assistance! Ask your sidekick to test you.
- There are lots of games that can help improve memory, like the card game Pairs. Or how about the tray game? Ask your sidekick to place ten objects on a tray and cover them with a cloth. They should show you the objects for a minute before covering them up again. Try to recall all the objects you saw. As you get better, you should try this with more objects and reducing the time you have to look at them.

 Read it and weep: Kim Peek, the guy who inspired the film *Rain Man*, could read books superfast and then remember every word. He could apparently read two pages at the same time, the left page with the left eye and the right page with the right. Give it a try yourself.

Photographic Memory **Form**

Once you have mastered this **Way to Become a Superhero**,
stick your Achieved Star here and fill in the form

Achieved

MEMORY TESTS

Ask your sidekick to secretly place 10 items on a tray and then cover them with a cloth. When you're ready, your sidekick should reveal the items for 60 seconds while you attempt to memorize the objects. When time is up and the tray has been covered again, see if you can remember all the objects. Write them in the space below. Then play the game again with new objects, but only give yourself 30 seconds to study them.

ATTEMPT 1 (60 secs)		ATTEMPT 2 (30 secs)	
Object 1	Object 6	Object 1	Object 6
Object 2	Object 7	Object 2	Object 7
Object 3	Object 8	Object 3	Object 8
Object 4	Object 9	Object 4	Object 9
Object 5	Object 10	Object 5	Object 10

How many did you get right after 60 seconds? [ ] / 10

How many did you get right after 30 seconds? [ ] / 10

How do you rate your memory?

☆ Awful   ☆ Poor
☆ Average   ☆ Good
☆ Excellent   ☆ Photo-graphic

For the second test, give yourself 60 seconds to study the contents of a room. When time's up, step outside and ask your sidekick to go in and remove one of the objects in there, replacing it with a new object. Return to the room and try to identify what has changed.

ATTEMPT 1	ATTEMPT 2
Write the new object here	Write the new object here
Write the missing object here	Write the missing object here
Did you get it right? y/n	Did you get it right? y/n

ATTEMPT 3	ATTEMPT 4
Write the new object here	Write the new object here
Write the missing object here	Write the missing object here
Did you get it right? y/n	Did you get it right? y/n

Did you use this power for...
GOOD? or
[ ] **EVIL?**
[ ]

At the same time you could master these other **Ways**:
5: Super-Vision • **63**: Observation Skills • **72**: Speak a Hundred Languages
80: Orientation

Withstand Heat and Cold

Your world-saving antics may take you to places with far more extreme climates than you're used to, so it would be wise to prepare for this. It certainly won't do to turn down work because "it's a bit cold out there."

Chill Out

- Extreme cold or heat can affect the brain, so listen to your body's warning signals and act fast before your mind's too addled to make good decisions. Always have plenty of water on you, as becoming dehydrated is a real danger whether toiling in hot or cold conditions.
- Protecting yourself from the sun, seeking out shade, and taking breaks whenever possible will help you cope with hot conditions. Don't eat large amounts, as this will increase your metabolism and you'll produce heat. Sweat is your friend and will cool you down (though you should replenish the moisture loss), as is loose clothing. Improve your tolerance of hot temperatures by sitting in a sauna—or taking a vacation in the tropics!
- In extreme cold, keep your head covered, as this is where you lose a lot of heat. At the same time it's important not to overheat, because then you sweat, and this moisture on your skin can cool you down. Stay dry and wear loose layers of clothing, which will form good insulation, and make sure the outer layer is waterproof. To improve your tolerance of cold temperatures, go skinny-dipping—or eat lots of ice cream!
- Design a couple of variations on your superhero outfit, or at least some accessories, to help you cope with challenging weather and climates.

One extreme to the other: Apart from inside an ice block from Mr. Freeze's cold gun, there is nowhere colder on Earth than the Antarctic or hotter than inside a volcano. But as survival in these places is so hard, it's unlikely any villain would use them as part of some evil plan.

Withstand Heat and Cold Form

Once you have mastered this **Way to Become a Superhero**, stick your Achieved Star here and fill in the form

Achieved

— FIRE AND ICE —

Make a note of your hottest and coldest experiences below, and from now on use the thermometer to record your record-breakingly cold and hot days. Take the quiz to find out how much you know about extreme temperatures. It's the sort of information that may well come in handy in your line of work.

— COLD —

What's the coldest temperature you've ever experienced?

`0 , 0` °F   Mark it on the thermometer

Where were you?

How did you keep warm?

— HOT —

What's the hottest temperature you've ever experienced?

`0 , 0` °F   Mark it on the thermometer

Where were you?

How did you keep cool?

— FEEL THE HEAT —

1. What temperature does water freeze at? `0 , 0` °F

2. What is our average core body temperature? `0 , 0` °F

3. At what core body temperature does hypothermia set in? `0 , 0` °F

Thermometer:
°F   °C
104 — 50
122 — 40
86 — 30
68 — 20
50 — 10
32 — 0
14 — -10
-4 — -20
-22 — -30
-40 — -40

4. What temperature is absolute zero? `– 0 , 0 , 0` °F

5. What's the lowest temperature ever recorded on Earth? `– 0 , 0` °F

6. Where was it recorded?

7. How cold is space? `– 0 , 0 , 0` °F

8. What temperature does water boil at? `0 , 0 , 0` °F

9. How hot is lava? `0 , 0 , 0 , 0 , 0` °F

10. Which is hotter, the surface of the sun or a lightning bolt?

Sun ☐   Lightning bolt ☐

11. What's the hottest temperature ever recorded on Earth? `0 , 0` °F

12. Where was it recorded?

Answers at the back of the book

Rate your ability to withstand . . .

. . . heat `out of 10`

. . . cold `out of 10`

Did you use this power for . . . **GOOD?** or **EVIL?**
☐ ☐

At the same time you could master these other **Ways**:
6: Stamina • **18**: Harness the Elements • **26**: Know Your Weaknesses
70: Cope Under Pressure • **72**: Speak a Hundred Languages • **90**: Healing

Take Risks

The trick is to assess the danger to yourself and others first. Of course, the whole point of risk-taking is that it's a bit of a gamble. However, there is such a thing as calculated risk. It's a brave but stupid superhero who dives into the sea to rescue someone even though they can't swim.

Bet Your Life

- You may have heard of SWOT analysis (Strengths, Weaknesses, Opportunities, Threats), used to calculate risk. The other method is FART: For, Against, Reality, Theory. In other words, before you take a risk, consider what factors will help you succeed (e.g., your skill, weather, having the right equipment, feeling positive) against the factors that will hinder you (e.g., aliens, giant spiders, evil villains). It's time to weigh the theoretical chances of success against the realistic outcome. Take the total number of "For" factors and subtract the total number of "Against" factors. If you end up with a positive number, the outlook is good—the higher the number the greater the risk worth taking. If you end up with a minus number, prepare to fail.

- Taking risks takes guts. You have to build up to superhero status by taking small measured risks to begin with, preferably with some incentive to spur you on. Make a list of ten things you'd like to do but have always been too scared to try. Mark them out of ten using the FART analysis. Then give the ones with the highest marks a try, gradually moving on to those where the risks are greater.

 "There was a young man from Bengal / Who went to a fancy-dress ball. / He thought he would risk it / And go as a biscuit, / But a dog ate him up in the hall." This well-known limerick contains a salutary lesson about risk: always factor in the unexpected.

Take Risks **Form**

Once you have mastered this **Way to Become a Superhero**, stick your Achieved Star here and fill in the form

Achieved

F.A.R.T. ANALYSIS

Next time you're faced with a risky decision, try the **F.A.R.T.** analysis below to assess your chances. First take a guess at your chance of success (in THEORY). Then think of as many factors FOR and AGAINST a successful outcome as you can, and when you've finished, do the math described below to turn this information into a percentage that represents your chances of success in REALITY.

Risk 1		Risk 2	
IN THEORY I have [ ] % chance of success		IN THEORY I have [ ] % chance of success	
FOR (+1)	**AGAINST (+1)**	**FOR (+1)**	**AGAINST (+1)**
TOTAL [ ]	TOTAL [ ]	TOTAL [ ]	TOTAL [ ]

Now do the following math: $\dfrac{\text{(FOR} - \text{AGAINST)}}{\text{(FOR} + \text{AGAINST)}} \times 100$

IN REALITY I have [ ] % chance of success

Which % was higher? Theory [ ] Reality [ ]

Did you decide to take this risk? [y/n]

If yes, what happened?

Now do the following math: $\dfrac{\text{(FOR} - \text{AGAINST)}}{\text{(FOR} + \text{AGAINST)}} \times 100$

IN REALITY I have [ ] % chance of success

Which % was higher? Theory [ ] Reality [ ]

Did you decide to take this risk? [y/n]

If yes, what happened?

Did you use this power for...
GOOD? or
[ ] EVIL? [ ]

At the same time you could master these other **Ways**:
13: Conquer Your Fears • **16**: Sixth Sense • **44**: Never Give Up • **50**: Second Sight
54: Make Sacrifices • **70**: Cope Under Pressure

Save the World from the Undead

Zombies, vampires, evil spirits, skeletons, and mummies all have one thing in common—they're fiendishly difficult to kill because they're already dead.

Don't Give Up the Ghost

- Some species of the undead are easier to spot than others. Skeletons, for example, are useless at disguise or creeping up on victims, and so prefer surprise attacks. Bullets and blades may prove ineffective, but a big club or catapult will have them in pieces. Mummies, also conspicuous, can be unraveled if you're nimble—and they're flammable.
- Vampires are experts at deception. They look like humans, only exceptionally attractive ones, so people are easily lured into their trap. Traditionally the best way to dispose of them is a stake in the heart, but to be triply sure you should cut off their heads and burn their bodies.
- Zombies are slow, uncoordinated, and sensitive to light, but one bite is all it takes to become infected—so their strength lies in their numbers. Long-range weapons and strong protective armor are recommended.
- Most ghosts are harmless and should be left alone, but an evil spirit can be extremely dangerous, as they're entirely without substance and will happily inhabit the bodies of innocent people. Getting rid of them requires detective work to find out what their grievance is and what can be done to lay their troubled souls to rest. A crucifix, holy water, and a Bible may help defensively but cannot be fully relied upon.

Damned if you do: Due to the drastic measures required to kill the undead, your ghoul's identity must be beyond doubt before proceeding, or else you risk eternal damnation yourself by getting the wrong guy. You need nerves of steel to wait until the last possible moment.

Save the World . . .
from the Undead **Form**

Once you have mastered this **Way to Become a Superhero**,
stick your Achieved Star here and fill in the form

Achieved

UNDEAD

— KNOW YOUR ENEMY —

The undead rely heavily on the element of surprise when it comes to attack,
so it's vital to be able to detect them early so you can implement your plan
of action.

Name of suspect

Enemy weaknesses

Which of the following telltale signs do they
exhibit?

Walking slowly
or floating

Transparency

Enemy strengths

Dead eyes

Bloodthirsty
dietary habits

Moaning

Unusual dress
sense

What do you suspect them of being?

A vampire   A skeleton   A zombie

A ghost   An evil
spirit   A mummy

YOU NEED A PLAN OF ACTION. WILL YOU . . .	Explain how you will carry out your plan below
. . . interrogate your suspect? — y/n	
. . . report your suspect? — y/n	
. . . neutralize your suspect? — y/n	
. . . recruit your suspect? — y/n	
. . . surrender to your suspect? — y/n	

Place a photo of
your undead suspect here

Did you use
this power for . . .
GOOD? or
EVIL?

At the same time you could master these other **Ways**:
16: Sixth Sense • **27**: See in the Dark • **38**: Assemble Your Armies of Darkness • **49**: Hone
Your Moral Compass • **52**: Telekinesis • **66**: Agility • **69**: Kung-Fu Master • **90**: Healing

Write the name of your restricted area here

WARNING!
NO UNAUTHORIZED
PERSONNEL

Locate Your Secret Base

A superhuman's home is his castle—or cave or tree house or bedroom. Wherever it is, your base should be a place where you can conduct operations without fear of exposure or attack. So before you get carried away with wallpaper samples, make sure the practical matters are covered.

Location, Location, Location

- Secrecy is key to security. If the location of your headquarters is unknown to others, you shouldn't have too much to worry about. Keeping it secret may be difficult, though. If your base is disguised as something else (like a bedroom), make sure that it can be converted at a moment's notice and that no clues lie strewn about to betray your true identity. You must learn the art of concealment.
- Your secret base must have enough storage space for your costume and equipment, including any supertransport. You'll also need a laboratory area in which to design, make, and test your gadgets.
- Can you get to your base quickly? There's no point in having all your stuff stashed away in a place that you can't reach in an emergency. Think about access and, in a worst-case scenario, secret escape routes and other hiding places to keep spare equipment.
- As the nerve center of your operations, your secret base should be set up so that you can keep a close eye on what's going on outside. Internet, television, radio, newspapers—these communication tools will be crucial for surveillance.

Home sweet home: Pay attention to the look and feel of your base too. It is to be your refuge and your fortress—somewhere you can relax and let the real you, the superhero/evil genius you, hang out, either with your sidekick or alone when you need to brood.

Locate Your Secret Base **Form**

Once you have mastered this **Way to Become a Superhero**, stick your Achieved Star here and fill in the form

Achieved

YOUR OWN AREA 51

Area 51 is a US military base in the heart of the Nevada desert. Although the site isn't a secret, no one knows what goes on inside. Conspiracy theories abound—most famously that a crashed UFO is being stored there. Unlike Area 51, you must keep the location of your base very secret. Don't write it down here—but do draw a plan of the layout below, checking off the listed features you include and adding your own.

☐ Filing cabinets

☐ World map

☐ Secret escape route

☐ Control desk and chair

☐ Costume closet

☐ Safe

☐ Design workshop

☐ Security systems

☐ Supertransport bay

☐ Armory

☐ Interrogation room

☐ Communications console and monitors

☐ Science lab

What else did you include?

If you're unable to keep your base hidden from the prying eyes of family and friends, make a sign similar to that on the opposite page (or photocopy and enlarge that one) to stick on the door to your secret HQ.

Did you use this power for...

GOOD? or

☐ **EVIL?**

☐

At the same time you could master these other **Ways**:
32: Get a Villainous Chair • **47**: Master of Illusion • **76**: Devise an Escape Plan • **79**: Design Your Own Gadgets • **86**: Keep Supersecrets • **97**: Know What's Happening Everywhere

Superhearing

Have you ever heard a pin drop, a butterfly sigh, or a flea sneeze? Probably not, which means you need to train those lugholes of yours until they're as sharp as a cat's. How else will you be able to eavesdrop on scheming villains or detect distress calls on the other side of town? Superhearing is not just about hearing better, but listening better too. Have you ever missed what someone's saying when they've been standing right beside you because your mind is elsewhere? Listen up now . . .

Superhearo

- Assess your current hearing abilities so you can monitor your improvement. Why don't you see if you can actually hear a pin drop or follow a conversation going on in the next room?
- Listen to silence, and listen hard. Then make a list of everything you heard, from the rumbling of your tummy to any sort of electrical static or gurgling pipes to birds singing to the wind and mice in the attic.
- Now listen to a multi-instrumental piece of music. See if you can focus on each instrument in turn and hum back what they're playing. You'll know when you're getting supergood because you can hum the second oboe part in Beethoven's Fifth Symphony!
- Learn to lip-read. The easiest way to practice is to sit in front of the TV with the sound turned down. Before you start, you might want to spend some time studying how your own mouth moves as you speak by sitting in front of a mirror and going through the alphabet.

Lend me your ears: As we get old, the hair cells in our inner ears begin to malfunction, which causes hearing loss, beginning with high-pitched sounds. Exposure to loud noise can damage these cells too, so start sticking your fingers in your ears rather than headphones.

Superhearing **Form**

Once you have mastered this **Way to Become a Superhero**, stick your Achieved Star here and fill in the form

Achieved

HEAR, HEAR!

Stop whatever you're doing and listen to the world around you. Timing yourself for one minute, list all the sounds you can hear.

Sound 1	Sound 2	Sound 3

Sound 4	Sound 5	Sound 6

Sound 7	Sound 8	Sound 9

Sound 10	Sound 11	Sound 12

Try this again blindfolded. Did you find your hearing became sharper when you couldn't see? y/n

READ MY LIPS

Even better than being able to hear small sounds is interpreting no sound at all. Reading lips is incredibly difficult, but if you can master it, then you'll be able to "hear" conversations across a room. Study the shape your mouth makes in a mirror as you produce the vowel sounds below. Draw the shape you see underneath them and memorize them to help you learn to lip-read. Then move on to other sounds—there are plenty more to learn!

A	E	I	O	U

NEXT-DOOR NEIGHBAWL

Listen to other people talking through a wall or door. Which method worked best? Number them in order of effectiveness:

Did you use this power for...

Cupping your hands around your ear

Listening through a glass held up against the wall

Using just your ear-power alone

GOOD? or

EVIL?

Approximately how much of the conversation could you pick up? 0 0 0 % Did you hear anything interesting? y/n

Were some voices harder to hear than others? If yes, why?

At the same time you could master these other **Ways**:

5: Super-Vision • **10**: Stealth • **16**: Sixth Sense • **34**: Supersmell

Observation Skills

It's important to be alert to suspicious behavior and unusual happenings at all times, but super-vision will be useless if you're not absorbing and processing what's in front of your eyes. You have to stop looking and start seeing. A clear mind helps so that you can concentrate on observing.

Eyes Wide Open

- Spot-the-difference puzzles are great for honing observation skills, but to get to superhero levels you'll need to be better than that. Take a good look around your bedroom, including inside cupboards and drawers. Ask your sidekick to move three objects while you step outside for a moment. See if you can spot what has changed. Do the same exercise in a room you're not familiar with.
- Take your sidekick to a shopping district and ask them to go inside a cafe or shop and take a digital photo of the interior while you wait outside. Once they have their photo, go inside and give yourself three minutes to absorb as much visual information as you can. When you come out, get your sidekick to ask you questions about their photo, including small details, like what people are drinking or wearing, or what color items are and how many there are.
- To test yourself properly, you need to be able to stay vigilant even when you're busy doing something else. So how about doing the test above, but this time get your sidekick to ask you math questions during your three-minute observation time?

Artful eyes: Art lovers can have fun practicing observation: copy masterpieces and draw still lifes (make it harder by looking for a few minutes, then drawing from memory), or visit galleries and look out for all the small details in paintings that other people might miss.

Observation Skills **Form**

Once you have mastered this **Way to Become a Superhero**, stick your Achieved Star here and fill in the form

Achieved

————— SPOT THE DIFFERENCE —————

Test your powers of observation with this spot-the-difference challenge. What six things have been changed in the second picture? Answers at the back of the book.

Difference 1

Difference 2

Difference 3

Difference 4

Difference 5

Difference 6

Did you use this power for...

GOOD? or

☐ **EVIL?**

☐

At the same time you could master these other **Ways**:
5: Super-Vision • **16**: Sixth Sense • **20**: Learn to Multitask • **27**: See in the Dark
40: Understand Body Language • **57**: Photographic Memory • **77**: X-Ray Vision

HISTORICAL SUPERFACTS

WRITE YOUR SUPERHERO
NAME HERE

THE TIME-TRAVELING
SUPERHERO LIVED HERE IN
1716, 1896, 2011,
3074 & 9012

Travel in Time

Time travel is an exceptionally risky business because, as every superhero knows, it creates paradoxes. If you travel back in time to change the future, the ripple effect from your interference may alter all sorts of things that should never have been meddled with. In short, it is to be avoided except in absolute emergencies, which is just as well, since it's not easy to do.

How Time Flies

- One quick and easy way to travel in time (though not cheap) is to hop on a plane and cross some time zones. So if you need to be somewhere yesterday, get on a plane and travel west. Hopefully you can achieve whatever it is you were hoping to achieve wherever it is you end up. Conversely, to travel into the future, you need to fly east.
- Sometimes it is not the actual traveling back or forward in time you need, but creating the illusion that this has happened. This will require some sneaky clock-changing behind people's backs. It's one of the oldest tricks in the book, but it's one of the best.
- Inventing a time machine is your only real chance of acquiring this special power. Einstein worked out that time would appear to slow down if you traveled really, really fast, but flying at the speed of light probably isn't worth the risk when there are easier ways to fake it (see above). Scientists have theorized about the time-traveling possibilities of black holes and wormholes in space, so if you want to explore those you'll need to get your head into some serious physics books.

 Time-traveling tips: Don't meet yourself. Don't kill your grandpa (i.e., the grandfather paradox: this would mean certain death for you). Dress appropriately. Know how to get back. Don't forget to take last night's winning lottery numbers with you. Leave nothing behind.

Travel in Time **Form**

Once you have mastered this **Way to Become a Superhero**, stick your Achieved Star here and fill in the form

Achieved

PAST, PRESENT, FUTURE

If you could travel back in time, what would you choose to change in your own life? What historical event would you alter to make the world a better place in your eyes? And what would you hope to find in the future?

PAST CARING

What year in your past would you like to travel back to? `0 0 0 0`

How old were you? `0 0`

What happened in your life in this year that you would like to change?

WARNING! Changing a past event will set off a chain reaction of consequences — think them through . . .

How would things be different today?

FUTURE PROOF

What year in your future would you like to travel forward to? `0 0 0 0`

How old will you be? `0 0`

Why are you interested in this year?

WARNING! Seeing your destiny could cause all manner of psychological problems . . .

What would you hope to find?

What would you dread finding?

PRESENT TENSE

Which past world event would you change if you could?

How would the world be different today?

When did this take place? `0 0 0 0`

Did you use this power for . . .
GOOD? or
☐ **EVIL?**
☐

At the same time you could master these other **Ways**:
29: Solve Impossible Problems • **33**: Anticipate Your Enemy's Next Move
36: Be in Two Places at Once • **39**: Speed • **47**: Master of Illusion • **50**: Second Sight

Talk Your Way Out of Trouble

It's usually the bad guys who don't know when to shut up, often because they can't resist boasting or being a smart-ass, or because they lack any social awareness, or, worse still, are just plain insane. Superheroes, on the other hand, are more likely to be the strong, silent type, and can generally get by with a few devastating one-liners. Generally.

Talk the Talk

- Devise convincing excuses to pull out at the drop of a hat for those times you're called away in an emergency. You should also practice apologizing to friends and family for all your sudden disappearances.
- Off-duty, you must restrain yourself around those who try to provoke or bully you. You can't show your physical dominance without giving the game away. By responding calmly, especially when someone's shouting angrily at you, you can bring the situation back under your control.
- You may need the gift of gab to persuade someone to do (or not do) something. Keeping mum and hoping for the best isn't a good idea.
- Talking can sometimes provide a handy distraction, allowing you to play for time with your enemy while you wait for backup to arrive or some other event to take place. Or you may need to coax them into talking while you continue (sneakily) to thwart their plans.
- Join a debate club to improve your confidence and to get you thinking on your feet and finding the best words to put your message across. Acting classes will also help you with your delivery and improvisation.

Quote, unquote: A great speaker can intimidate, inspire, persuade, captivate . . . and change the course of history. Look at the example (both good and bad) of people like William Wilberforce; Winston Churchill; Hitler; Martin Luther King, Jr.; and John F. Kennedy.

Talk Your Way Out of Trouble **Form**

Once you have mastered this **Way to Become a Superhero**,
stick your Achieved Star here and fill in the form

Achieved

———— ORDER! ORDER! ————

Talking your way out of trouble will be a lot easier once you've mastered the art of winning arguments. Pick a controversial topic to debate with a friend or family member and see who can give you a run for your money.

TOPIC FOR DEBATE
Complete the sentence below with a statement of belief.

> I believe that . . .

FOR	**AGAINST**	**COUNTER**
List the main points backing your argument	List the likely arguments your opponent will use against you	List the points you can make to counter their arguments

Who won the argument?

You ☐   Did you learn anything new? [y/n] — If yes, what? [   ]

Your opponent ☐   Could you see both sides of the argument? [y/n]   How well do you think you debated?

It was a draw ☐   Has the debate changed your belief? [y/n]   ☆☆☆☆☆
Badly Okay Well Very well Excellently

— BRING IT ON! —

Find another opponent and debate the topic again, but this time argue against your statement of belief. This will really hone your skills and make you examine the issue from all sides.

Who won the argument?

You ☐   Your opponent ☐   It was a draw ☐

How well do you think you debated?

☆☆☆☆☆
Badly Okay Well Very well Excellently

Did you use this power for. . . .
GOOD? ☐ or
EVIL? ☐

At the same time you could master these other **Ways**:
8: Kick Ass Humanely • **22**: Communicate with Animals • **56**: Invent Some
Great One-Liners • **86**: Keep Supersecrets • **93**: Develop Powers of Persuasion

Agility

Agility is all about combining balance with speed, strength, and coordination, so really it's four skills in one. If you're chasing someone through a busy street or a forest (or being chased), you need to be fast and you need to be steady on your feet. Your life may depend on it.

Best Foot Forward

- It's not just a physical challenge but a mental one—you need to make quick decisions and react at lightning speed. Start your training off at a carnival on the bumper cars, but rather than trying to crash into other cars, you should focus all your efforts on getting through unbumped.
- One form of activity that will help build your skill in all four areas is dancing, particularly tap or street dance. If you were born without rhythm, try jumping rope instead.
- Practice sprinting and stopping suddenly (in two steps), holding your balance in the stopped position for ten seconds. Practice turning as you run too, pivoting on the balls of your feet rather than running in an arc. Get some friends together for a game of dodgeball.
- With a piece of chalk, find a safe area (like a playground) to mark out a ladder with at least eight rungs. Devise some drills that get you from one end of the ladder to the other using jumping and/or hopping. You can jump forward, backward, and sideways, using the insides of the boxes as well as either side of the ladder. Speed is of the essence. Ask your sidekick to time you in training with a stopwatch.

Not a leg to stand on: When you've had enough of all this running around, try standing still—on one leg, like a stork. It's not the most interesting exercise but it'll strengthen your leg muscles and improve your balance. Also practice headstands and handstands.

Agility Form

Once you have mastered this **Way to Become a Superhero**,
stick your Achieved Star here and fill in the form

Achieved

ASSAULT & BATTERIES

To be a successful superhero you need to be more agile than your enemy. Build your own obstacle
course and see how quickly you can complete it.

Which of the following skills did your course test?

Jumping	Skipping	Burrowing	Scrambling	Dodging
Swinging	Shooting	Running	Tunneling	Climbing
Sliding	Crawling	Balancing	Swimming	Other

If other, what else was featured in your course?   What were the hardest parts of your course?

How long did it take to complete your course?

Attempt 1   Attempt 2   Attempt 3
0,0 mins 0,0 secs   0,0 mins 0,0 secs   0,0 mins 0,0 secs

Draw in the various obstacles you set along your course

START
1.   2.   3.

6.   5.   4.

7.   8.

10.   9.

11.   12.

FINISH
14.   13.

*Did you use
this power for...*
GOOD? *or*
EVIL?

At the same time you could master these other **Ways**:
10: Stealth • **21**: Dexterity • **36**: Be in Two Places at Once • **39**: Speed • **43**: Invisibility
83: Hand–Eye Skill

Select a Call Signal

Superman may have ducked into the odd phone booth, but it wasn't to answer calls. You're not another option on the 911 emergency services— you're an ass-kicking mysterious caped crusader. Having a phone number or an e-mail address that folks in distress can use to contact you will only encourage those same people to lodge complaints when they don't like the service they're getting. Think of a way for the people of your village, town, or city to get ahold of you without blowing your cover.

Call On Me

- If you want to model your signal on Batman's searchlight, you'll need to design a logo that will work in silhouette. As a test, cut out a small version in cardboard, lay it against a powerful flashlight, and shine it on the ceiling of a darkened room. If you continue down this route, you'll be limited to working nights, and cloudy nights at that. Still, it'll look cool and help to strike terror into the hearts of villains. Alternatively, if you're a whiz with wires, you could design some sort of remote control button that sets off a flashing red light in your secret base.

- If you're musical, why not compose a theme tune for yourself that can be blared out of loudspeakers whenever your assistance is required? Your theme should be awe-inspiring and arresting, so don't go for anything too poptastic or cheerful. It needs to be good enough so that people won't mind hearing it again and again, but short and dramatic so that they don't forget it is an alarm call as they sing along.

Call your bluff: Don't rush off to answer your distress signal without being prepared for danger when you arrive. Batman was caught out by criminals who used his Bat Signal as a way of luring the superhero into a trap. You should keep your wits about you at all times.

Select a Call Signal **Form**

Once you have mastered this **Way to Become a Superhero**, stick your Achieved Star here and fill in the form

Achieved

— CALL ME —

What sort of call signal will you devise?

A searchlight projection ☐

A button-operated alarm ☐

A jingle to be played over loudspeakers ☐

If other, please specify

☐

If you go for the projection, draw a silhouette version of your logo (see **Way to Become a Superhero** No. 24) in the searchlight below.

If you went for a musical jingle, write the lyrics in the space provided below.

If you're familiar with musical notation, write the tune of your jingle in the score below.

Whatever type of call signal you go for, you will have to decide where to put it or whom to give it to. Responsible use of your call signal is very important. You won't have time to respond to false alarms or deal with petty problems. Will you . . .

. . . give it to the chief of police? y/n

. . . give it to the mayor or other town council official? y/n

. . . put it in a central public location in town? y/n

If yes, where exactly would you place it?

Did you use this power for . . .

GOOD? or ☐

EVIL? ☐

If other, please specify

At the same time you could master these other **Ways**:
2: Choose Your Name • **18**: Harness the Elements • **24**: Design a Logo
48: Choose a Calling Card • **79**: Design Your Own Gadgets

Survive Your Fatal Flaw

When it comes down to it, all the money, technology, and weapons in the world cannot stop the grinding wheels of Fate from bearing down on you. If you're lucky you'll be able to jump out of the way and make a swift exit. If you're not, it's the asylum or, worse still, a gruesomely spectacular death. Your fatal flaw is the one thing you can be sure will let you down. The good news is that superheroes suffer from a similar condition. The bad news is that they have an annoying habit of overcoming theirs.

Put Your Foot to the Flaw

- An evil genius's fatal flaw is often the very thing that makes them brilliant, and that's why you're doomed from the start. Greed is a classic example. In fact, a glance down the list of seven deadly sins is a good place to start looking for your fatal flaw.
- The only thing that can really save you from yourself is someone who loves you—someone willing to take the heat for you and allow you to cheat death by stepping into your place. What kind of sap would do that for a monster like you? Find this sap and nurture their love.
- This is all very tragic. There is another way, though. A fatal flaw can also be countered by a redeeming feature. You'll have to look very hard indeed for this one. It'll go against all your basest instincts to tease out the good in you, and when you've done it you'll have to hope your superhero nemesis is stupid enough to believe you have turned your back on your evil for good. Sucker.

A morality tale: Naive people would say Anakin Skywalker's anger was his fatal flaw, as it turned him into Darth Vader. Of course, this was actually his strong point. His real flaw was his love for his son. In saving Luke, he ended up dying himself. Love is toxic. Beware.

Survive Your Fatal Flaw **Form**

Once you have mastered this **Way to Become an Evil Genius**,
stick your Achieved Star here and fill in the form

Achieved

IT'S YOUR FAULT

Draw or name your fatal flaw in the
space provided below . . .

List all your other
weaknesses below . . .

Draw or name your one redeeming
feature in the label below . . .

**DANGER
OF DEATH**

ANTIDOTE

SHOW YOUR FLAW THE DOOR

Name someone you think would give up their
life to save you.

Do other people know about your fatal flaw or
have you managed to keep it under wraps?

It's a heavily guarded secret.

Would you give up your life for them?   y/n

Only those closest to me know about it.

If yes, beware. This could prove your fatal flaw.

Unfortunately, it's common knowledge.

Has your fatal flaw ever gotten you into
trouble before?   y/n

Do you know your enemy's fatal flaw?   y/n

If yes, how did you survive?

If yes, how can you exploit it?

At the same time you could master these other **Ways**:
11: Groom Your Dark Side • **33**: Anticipate Your Enemy's Next Move
59: Take Risks • **76**: Devise an Escape Plan • **100**: Devise Your Villainous Comeback

Kung-Fu Master

If you learn just one type of combat, let it be from the kung-fu school. There are hundreds of styles, many inspired by animals or Chinese philosophy, and all aim not only to hone self-defense skills but also to encourage self-cultivation of mind, spirit, and body. It's more than just clever moves—it's a way of life.

State-of-the-Martial-Art

- A key concept in many forms of kung fu (but chiefly Shaolin) is that of "qi" (pronounced "chee"). Think of it like the Force in *Star Wars*—an energy that exists all around us and in every living thing and that can be transformed from breath into movement. Try to feel the "qi" and use it. Meditation and yoga can help you with this.
- Every kung-fu pupil needs a master, so find a local class to join. "Kung fu" means "skill achieved with great effort," so you need to be dedicated. There are "hard" styles, which focus on directing energy outward into power strikes and blocks, and "soft" ones, which focus more on internal energy and redirecting the momentum of an attack so as to unbalance an opponent; some styles concentrate on upper body, some on lower. Choose one that covers it all—you can't afford to have any weak spots.
- Once you're on your way to becoming a kung-fu master you can develop your own style. What will be your inspiration? Your identity as a superhero or villain and the other superpowers you possess that make you unique should suggest something to you. Perhaps your superhero pose can be based on one of your own moves.

 Kung-fu masters on film: For an education in kung fu from the comfort of your sofa, watch Bruce Lee's *Fist of Fury* and *Enter the Dragon*, Jackie Chan's *Drunken Master* and *Snake in the Eagle's Shadow,* and Jet Li's *Once Upon a Time in China* series and *Hero*.

Kung-Fu Master Form

Once you have mastered this **Way to Become a Superhero**, stick your Achieved Star here and fill in the form

Achieved

KING KUNG

Take photos of you and your sidekick posing in kung-fu stances you've come up with yourselves. Don't let your sidekick cramp your style—they should develop their own.

YOUR MOVES

Place a photo of your attack stance here

Name of move here

Place a photo of your defense stance here

Name of move here

Place a photo of your favorite move here

Name of move here

YOUR SIDEKICK'S MOVES

Place a photo of their attack stance here

Name of move here

Place a photo of their defense stance here

Name of move here

Rate your kung-fu skills

☆ Awful ☆ Poor ☆ Average
☆ Good ☆ Very good ☆ Excellent

Did you use this power for...
GOOD? or
☐ **EVIL?**
☐

At the same time you could master these other **Ways**:
8: Kick Ass Humanely • **10**: Stealth • **14**: Strength • **16**: Sixth Sense • **25**: Control Your Temper • **28**: Balance • **42**: Strike a Superhero Pose • **66**: Agility • **83**: Hand–Eye Skill

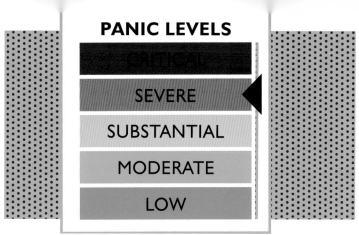

PANIC LEVELS

CRITICAL

SEVERE

SUBSTANTIAL

MODERATE

LOW

Cope Under Pressure

People deal with stress in different ways. If there isn't time in your world-saving schedule to take a coffee break, you'll need to find another way. Ultimately, the solution is to remove the cause of your stress quickly and effectively. For this, you must focus on the task and shut out the voices of doubt and anxiety that interfere with your ability to perform.

Keep Calm and Carry On

- You can combat stress by breathing slowly, deeply, and evenly. Yoga and meditation are both great ways to learn this properly.
- Any kind of time-trial challenge will get your adrenaline racing and notch up the pressure. Ask your sidekick to give you a variety of challenges—some mental, some physical, some both—and to give you strict time limits within which to complete each challenge.
- Audition for something. It could be a competition, a play, a choir, a TV show—whatever it is, there is nothing more unnerving than performing in front of other people with the weight of expectation upon you.
- If you play team sports, always offer to take the penalties when they come up. This is an excellent method to get yourself used to high-pressure win-or-lose situations. Being up for the challenge is half the battle. We've all seen what can happen in a penalty shoot-out when nerves get the better of even the greatest players.
- Get used to deadlines, especially short ones. Volunteer to work on a small newspaper or magazine.

 Soothing the savage beast: Listening to music can lift the spirits and drown out nagging doubts—nothing too dreary or melancholy, please. Help your body to cope with stress too by drinking plenty of water and eating healthy snacks to keep your energy levels up.

Cope Under Pressure **Form**

Once you have mastered this **Way to Become a Superhero**, stick your Achieved Star here and fill in the form

Achieved

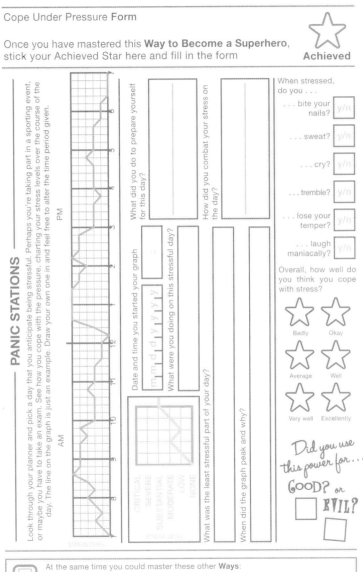

PANIC STATIONS

Look through your planner and pick a day that you anticipate being stressful. Perhaps you're taking part in a sporting event, or maybe you have to take an exam. See how you cope with the pressure, charting your stress levels over the course of the day. The line on the graph is just an example. Draw your own one in and feel free to alter the time period given.

AM   PM

STRESS LEVEL

CRITICAL
SEVERE
SUBSTANTIAL
MODERATE
LOW
NONE

What did you do to prepare yourself for this day?

How did you combat your stress on the day?

Date and time you started your graph

m m / d d / y y y y

What were you doing on this stressful day?

What was the least stressful part of your day?

When did the graph peak and why?

When stressed, do you . . .

. . . bite your nails? y/n

. . . sweat? y/n

. . . cry? y/n

. . . tremble? y/n

. . . lose your temper? y/n

. . . laugh maniacally? y/n

Overall, how well do you think you cope with stress?

Badly   Okay

Average   Well

Very well   Excellently

Did you use this power for . . .

GOOD? or

☐ EVIL?

☐

At the same time you could master these other **Ways**:
6: Stamina • **13**: Conquer Your Fears • **25**: Control Your Temper • **44**: Never Give Up
59: Take Risks

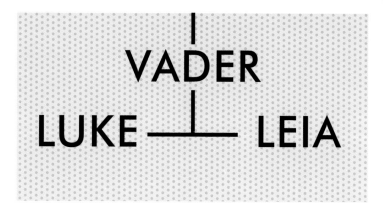

Trace Your Superhero Origins

Think back to the first time you had an inkling of your own destiny. Did it gradually dawn on you or did you experience a profound life-changing moment that opened your eyes to your superhuman potential?

Inherit the Earth

- If you were born with superpowers you'll want to find out if you've inherited these gifts. It doesn't necessarily mean your mom and dad are closet superheroes—you could be a freak of nature—but don't discount this theory until you've conducted close observation.
- Investigate your family history. Your relations will be thrilled you're taking an interest and happy to assist without asking awkward questions. It takes a lot of work to research a family tree—it'll be even harder to uncover your family's best-kept secrets. Start by finding out what kind of jobs your ancestors had, where they lived, and what kind of people they were. If you find you had a reclusive great-uncle who lived in a castle and was an inventor, focus on him.
- If you've done your family research and still can't find the answers, you'll have to craft your own backstory. Write a short narrative explaining how you came to have such unique abilities. Was it a freak accident (such as being struck by lightning) or a scientific experiment gone wrong? Did something terrible happen to you when you were little that made you determined to crusade for justice in your own special way? What made you first don that mask (if you have one)?

 Skeletons in the closet: As you dig around in your family's past, you may uncover all sorts of dark secrets. If there's evidence of a strong line of villainy going back generations, it's good to be aware of this so you can fortify your mind against any sudden evil impulses.

Trace Your Superhero Origins **Form**

Once you have mastered this **Way to Become a Superhero**,
stick your Achieved Star here and fill in the form

Achieved

ORIGINS AND LEMONS

Look into your family history and try to uncover clues to your superhuman origins. It could be an
ancestor who survived against the odds or who went mysteriously missing . . .

THE PAST

Year of birth	Name of family member	Clues to superhuman status
0 0 0 0		
Year of death*	Relationship to you	
0 0 0 0		

Year of birth	Name of family member	Clues to superhuman status
0 0 0 0		
Year of death*	Relationship to you	
0 0 0 0		

Year of birth	Name of family member	Clues to superhuman status
0 0 0 0		
Year of death*	Relationship to you	
0 0 0 0		

THE PRESENT—YOUR DETAILS

Year of your birth

0 0 0 0   Your superhero name here   List your inherited special powers here

If you're scraping the barrel trying to uncover superancestors, come up
with another theory for your superhuman talents.

It all began when . . .

Did you use this power for . . .

GOOD? or

☐ **EVIL?**

☐

*if applicable

At the same time you could master these other **Ways**:
1: Discover Your Alter Ego • **4**: Have a Twisted Backstory • **26**: Know Your Weaknesses
31: Identify Your Nemesis • **68**: Survive Your Fatal Flaw • **86**: Keep Supersecrets

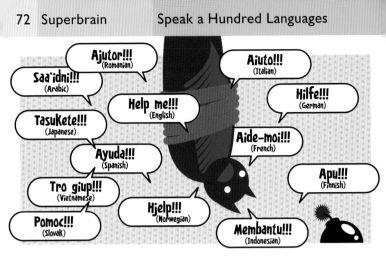

Speak a Hundred Languages

Your world-saving feats will take you to many countries, the most far-flung corners of the planet, and even beyond. Imagine how quickly your superhero actions will fall apart if you can't communicate with the public, with heads of state and security forces, and even with your enemy. How would you negotiate with the bad guys? How would you tell people to "RUN!"?

Tongue Tied

- You would ideally become fluent in all 67,000 Earth languages, but that's not going to happen overnight, of course. So concentrate on the most widely spoken world languages, and that should cover you in the majority of emergencies. Those languages are (in order): Mandarin, Arabic, English, Spanish, Bengali, Hindi, Portuguese, Russian, and Japanese. Some Latin and Ancient Greek and Hebrew might come in handy too for deciphering old manuscripts and ancient prophecies.

- Draw up a list of the key phrases you might need in emergencies, like: "Look behind you!"; "I'd rather die than beg for a small favor such as my life"; "This outrage will not go unavenged"; "There are bigger things happening here than me and you"; "Don't do it!" and "Did anyone see a big green fella with three heads go past here lately?" Learn to say them in your chosen languages.

- If all else fails, learn sign language. You may be called upon to act as an ambassador for your planet or fight alien invaders, and so an international, nonverbal kind of language could be just what you need.

More than you can chew: Don't think your work is done once you've mastered human languages. At times it may be necessary to communicate with nature, animals, technology— even the spirit world. You'd best get working on that photographic memory.

Speak a Hundred Languages **Form**

Once you have mastered this **Way to Become a Superhero**, stick your Achieved Star here and fill in the form

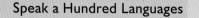

Achieved

--- **SUPERSIGNS** ---

Sign language is pretty universal. A thumbs-up can be understood in most places (although across the Middle East and parts of deep space it is an insult and could get you into real trouble). Invent your own super sign language for emergency situations that all races will be able to interpret. Start with the phrases below—draw your specially designed hand signals in the boxes provided.

LOOK BEHIND YOU!	DANGER! TROUBLE AHEAD	YOU'RE GOING TO GET IT

I'M HERE TO SAVE YOU	I'M ARMED AND DANGEROUS	DON'T DO IT!

--- **LANGUAGE!** ---

It is probably wise to learn key phrases in some other languages too, just in case you can't be seen or are unable, for some reason, to gesticulate. Choose one of the phrases above and learn it in at least three different languages.

Your key phrase here

In language 1

Name the three languages here

In language 2

In language 3

Did you use this power for...

GOOD? or

☐ **EVIL?**

☐

At the same time you could master these other **Ways**:
3: Take Flight • **7**: Decipher Devious Riddles • **22**: Communicate with Animals • **23**: Plan for World Domination • **80**: Orientation • **97**: Know What's Happening Everywhere

Create a Force Field

There's only so much battering the human body can take, even the super-human body. Shields are unwieldy and limited in size and strength. To become truly invincible, you need to develop some kind of force field. Here are a few ideas to set you on a path of discovery.

Have a Field Day

- Start your investigations with this simple experiment. Ask your sidekick to stand with their hands held out in front of them, as if frozen in mid-clap. Place your hands between your sidekick's and slowly start to push out against them—they must resist the pressure at all costs, pushing in to keep your hands from moving apart. Keep going . . . After about 30 seconds your sidekick can lower their hands. Try bringing your hands together now. Can you feel a force field pushing them apart?
- Blow up two balloons and attach strings to both of them. Rub the balloons on your hair, then, holding the strings with one hand, let them float and see what happens. The balloons will have picked up electrons from your hair and become negatively charged, and materials with similar charges repel each other, so they'll move apart as if there's a force field between them. This is good to know should you ever be attacked by a bunch of balloons, but for wider use you'll need to do a little more research.
- If you've been working on your telekinesis powers you might be able to generate a force field with the power of your mind alone. Focus your efforts on manipulating the electromagnetic fields around us.

Highly implasmable: Where there's a superpower there's a team of scientists hunting for a scientific way of achieving it. With force fields, a lot of research has focused on plasma (gas that contains charged particles), which can get very thick and impenetrable when heated.

Create a Force Field **Form**

Once you have mastered this **Way to Become a Superhero**, stick your Achieved Star here and fill in the form

Achieved

FORCE FIELD GAME

OBJECT OF THE GAME: to defend the area within your force field by repelling missiles hurled at you by your sidekick.

WHAT YOU NEED: a sidekick • a large open area to play in • a ball of string • a long piece of chalk • sponges • a bucket of water • a shield of your choosing

1. Select a spot for the center of your area and mark out your force field in a circle around it. A good way to do this is to tie the end of a ball of string to a piece of chalk. Unravel the ball of string as long as you want the radius of your circular area to be, then ask your sidekick to hold the ball firmly on the middle spot, while you pull the length of string taut and chalk out a circle around them.

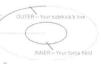

2. Once you've marked out your force field, ask your sidekick to let out more string from the ball so that you can mark out a bigger circle around it. This outer circle forms a boundary across which your sidekick must not step.

OUTER—Your sidekick's line
INNER—Your force field

3. Choose an object that you think will best deflect the wet sponge missiles. It might be a tray, a tennis racket, or an umbrella.

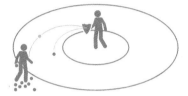

4. Stand in your area and use your shield to bat away the missiles your sidekick hurls at you. Your sidekick gets a point for any sponges that land within your force field. They get a bonus point for any that land a direct hit on you. You get a point every time you deflect a sponge out of your area. If one of your deflected sponges hits your sidekick, you get a bonus point. Who will get the wettest?

5. Once you've had a try at defending the central circle, switch places and be the missile hurler.

YOUR TURN

What did you use as a shield?

Write your scores below

You `0 0`   Your sidekick `0 0`

How wet did you get?

Not much	A bit	damp	Pretty wet	Soaking
☐	☐	☐	☐	☐

THEIR TURN

What did they use as a shield?

Write your scores below

You `0 0`   Your sidekick `0 0`

How wet did they get?

Not much	A bit	damp	Pretty wet	Soaking
☐	☐	☐	☐	☐

Did you use this power for... **GOOD?** or ☐ **EVIL?**

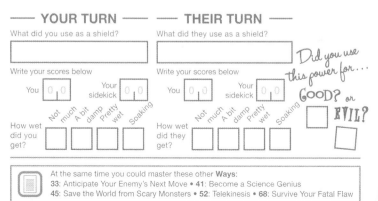

At the same time you could master these other **Ways:**
33: Anticipate Your Enemy's Next Move • **41:** Become a Science Genius
45: Save the World from Scary Monsters • **52:** Telekinesis • **68:** Survive Your Fatal Flaw

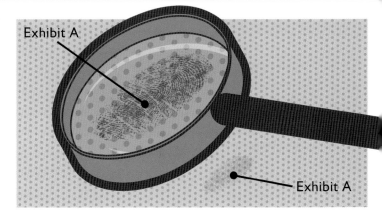

Exhibit A

Exhibit A

Identify and Interpret Clues

You can't always be ahead of the game, but just because you've arrived on the scene too late to save the day doesn't mean you've wasted your time. Detective work is a vital part of your job, so make sure you have the tools and skills for the task. Catch that slippery villain before he strikes again!

Clued-Up

- A crime scene must first be secured. Make sure nobody touches anything, and check in case your enemy is still around, hiding.
- Try to figure out where the villain entered and exited. Look for anything they may have left behind—footprints, scraps of paper or clothing, weapons—and take photos before bagging them up to take back for analysis. Your super-vision (or a magnifying glass) will help you find less obvious clues, like hairs, threads, scratches, and fingerprints. Try taking prints from smooth objects. There are instructions for fingerprinting on the opposite page.
- If you find any bits of written evidence, what are they telling you? If it's handwritten, analyze the writing and file it like a fingerprint in case you identify a match at some point.
- Round up any witnesses and question them (see **Way to Become a Superhero** No. 87). Will you play good cop or bad cop? Use your lie-detecting skills to get to the truth, and telepathy if you think a witness may be hiding something.
- Try to think like your enemy. How would they have escaped? What would their motives have been? Piece together a psychological profile.

Signature clues: Most supervillains are egomaniacs who love to publicize their crimes by leaving some form of calling card at the scene. If you find one, be sure to check it against any others you've gathered, in case you have a copycat criminal on your hands.

Identify and Interpret Clues **Form**

Once you have mastered this **Way to Become a Superhero**, stick your Achieved Star here and fill in the form

Achieved

FINE PRINT

Here's an easy way to take a fingerprint. Sprinkle fine dust (like flour or cocoa powder) over the fingerprint, then gently brush away the excess with a feather, leaving the dust that sticks to the grease. Place a piece of clear sticky tape over the print and press down, then carefully peel the tape away with the fingerprint left on it and stick it down onto a piece of cardboard.

Take a print from somewhere around your home and make an educated guess at whom it belongs to. Stick it in box A. Whom do you suspect?

Stick the print you took here · Your culprit's print here

| A | B |

Now, using an inkpad, take your suspect's fingerprints.

Did you find a perfect match?   y/n

If yes, get your culprit to print the guilty finger in box B.

DRAW YOUR CONCLUSIONS

Once you've gathered your evidence, you need to put together a story that links it all together. Next time you're at the scene of a crime, use the table below to help you analyze the clues you found.

Crime committed

Victim(s)

Location

Date m, m, d, d, y, y, y, y

Rate your detection skills

Bad · Okay

Average · Good

Very good · Excellent

Is there evidence of . . .	CLUES	CONCLUSIONS
. . . the method of entry/exit?		
. . . the time of the crime?		
. . . the villain's identity?		
. . . the villain's motive?		
. . . assistance from an insider or henchmen?		
. . . a search?		
. . . a struggle?		

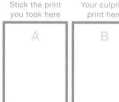

Did you use this power for . . .

GOOD? or ☐ **EVIL?** ☐

At the same time you could master these other **Ways**:
33: Anticipate Your Enemy's Next Move • **55**: Break Codes • **57**: Photographic Memory
63: Observation Skills • **87**: Interrogation • **89**: Know When Someone's Lying

Save the World from Environmental Disaster

It's probably the most talked about and highly anticipated threat to the planet, and while everyone can play their part to help reduce carbon emissions and waste, it will take superhuman effort to reverse the effects of deforestation, pollution, resource depletion, and global warming.

If You Can't Stand the Heat . . .

- . . . get off the planet. This is a worst-case scenario and requires a rather unsuperheroic "save yourself" attitude. Try the following options first.
- The power of nature is greater even than your superpowers at their peak. However, unlike most other types of enemy, you don't need to battle against nature but work with it. The best way to train for this is to find out as much as you can about the systems that keep life-on-Earth-as-we-know-it ticking, and to examine how it might be possible to achieve a balance between our needs and the needs of those systems. Research, observe, and learn. Knowledge is power.
- As always, leading by example is one of the most powerful methods. Show people there is plenty they can do to help in the effort. Gather your superteam and plan a publicity stunt that demonstrates energy-saving on an impressive level.
- As a superhero, more than anyone you should be able to demonstrate that you are self-sufficient. Make it your mission to rely as little as possible on anything that has not been produced by your good self. Monitor your waste and your recycling and keep trying to improve.

> **Global arming:** If global warming was a war, on one side you'd have an army of chimneys, on the other an army of trees. You need to recruit more soldiers, Captain Greenfingers. Get together with your sidekick and come up with a tree-planting scheme.

Save the World . . .
from Environmental Disaster **Form**

Once you have mastered this **Way to Become a Superhero**, stick your Achieved Star here and fill in the form

Achieved

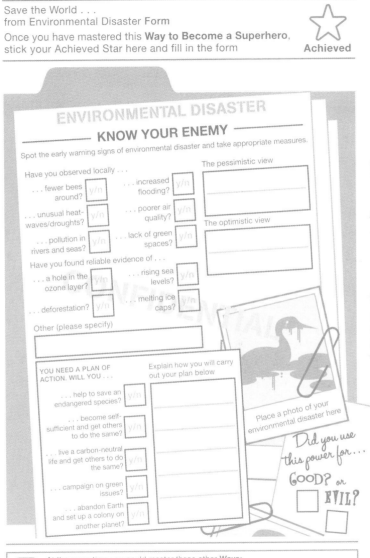

ENVIRONMENTAL DISASTER

— KNOW YOUR ENEMY —

Spot the early warning signs of environmental disaster and take appropriate measures.

Have you observed locally . . .

. . . fewer bees around? [y/n]

. . . increased flooding? [y/n]

. . . unusual heat-waves/droughts? [y/n]

. . . poorer air quality? [y/n]

. . . pollution in rivers and seas? [y/n]

. . . lack of green spaces? [y/n]

The pessimistic view

The optimistic view

Have you found reliable evidence of . . .

. . . a hole in the ozone layer? [y/n]

. . . rising sea levels? [y/n]

. . . deforestation? [y/n]

. . . melting ice caps? [y/n]

Other (please specify)

YOU NEED A PLAN OF ACTION. WILL YOU . . .

. . . help to save an endangered species? [y/n]

. . . become self-sufficient and get others to do the same? [y/n]

. . . live a carbon-neutral life and get others to do the same? [y/n]

. . . campaign on green issues? [y/n]

. . . abandon Earth and set up a colony on another planet? [y/n]

Explain how you will carry out your plan below

Place a photo of your environmental disaster here

Did you use this power for . . .

GOOD? or

EVIL?

At the same time you could master these other **Ways**:
18: Harness the Elements • **46**: Choose a Cause • **58**: Withstand Heat and Cold
63: Observation Skills • **78**: Be a Good Influence • **99**: Gather a Superteam

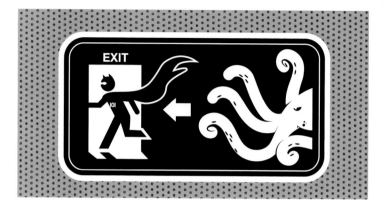

Devise an Escape Plan

Otherwise known as an "exit strategy," your escape plan is your ticket to freedom when the party's over. Success is not merely in the achieving of your vile aims, but in doing so without being caught, so you should mastermind your getaway as meticulously as the rest of your evil project, which means having a backup escape plan at the ready too.

Over and Out

- Wherever you happen to be controlling operations from, you must ensure that you have some form of transport on hand, preferably well concealed so that no one else can block your way to it or steal off in it themselves.
- Be ready to use some method of distraction when confronted by your foe, enabling you to sneak away to your hidden vehicle easily. One excellent way to stall a superhero on the verge of apprehending you is to put a new task in their way that will prove irresistible to their goody-goody urges. For example, if you reveal that the superhero's sweetheart is being lowered into your crocodile pond, saving him or her is more than likely to take priority over nabbing you.
- If a meddling superhero has intercepted your operation, there's every chance they've also learned the location of your secret HQ—or, worse still, destroyed it. You'll need an even-more-secret base to sit out the next few days while you take stock of your position and work out what to do next.

Floor planning: No matter where you are, it's vital you know all the ways in and out. Draw a plan of your HQ and any mission locations, marking all possible escape routes, and work out where to strategically place equipment, like ropes, to make escaping easier.

Devise an Escape Plan **Form**

Once you have mastered this **Way to Become an Evil Genius**,
stick your Achieved Star here and fill in the form

Achieved

--- **RUN AWAY!** ---

Escape from the scene of your crime and find your way to your secret base
without running into any meddling cops, superheroes, or nasty tentacled surprises.

At the same time you could master these other **Ways**:
10: Stealth • **33**: Anticipate Your Enemy's Next Move • **39**: Speed • **43**: Invisibility
61: Locate Your Secret Base • **63**: Observation Skills • **91**: Design Your Supertransport

X-Ray Vision

Some superheroes are born great, some achieve greatness, and others have greatness thrust upon them. If you weren't born with X-ray vision, and in spite of your best efforts you're unable to achieve it, you may just have to have that power thrust upon you—upon your face, more precisely—in the form of X-ray glasses.

I See Through You

- Check first that you can't do this naturally. Take a wall, any wall, and stare at it really hard. Try not to blink. Use your mind's eye to visualize what lies behind . . . No good? Okay, move on to step two.
- On the opposite page you'll find instructions on how to make a pair of X-ray glasses the traditional way. It may take some adjustment to get them working, but the basics are there and it's up to you, science genius, to refine the engineering and fashion them into a style that matches your look.
- Test your glasses for strength. Start with lightweight materials like paper and fabric, and work your way up through wood and plaster to metal and concrete, testing the effectiveness of your invention. True superheroes refrain from using their X-ray powers to check out people's underwear, though even they sometimes take an occasional peek.
- If your experiments prove a complete failure, you may have to resort to other methods to spy on your enemies on the other side of walls. Get ahold of some tiny mirrors, or highly reflective material, which you can slip under doors or attach to a rod and use to peer around corners.

No security blanket: The latest airport X-ray machines can check for hidden weapons by beaming electromagnetic waves at a passenger as they stand in a booth, to produce a virtual 3-D "naked" image of them. Unsurprisingly these scanners have proved rather controversial.

X-Ray Vision Form

Once you have mastered this **Way to Become a Superhero**, stick your Achieved Star here and fill in the form

Achieved

——— X-SPEX ———
YOU'LL NEED:

A pair of glasses, cardboard (a cereal box will do), scissors, a hole-punch, glue, a few feathers (fine white ones, from a pillow), markers/paint

WHAT TO DO:

1. Use a pair of your own glasses as a template, or, if you don't have any, trace around the template provided here. The important thing is that you have the front shape of a pair of glasses to lay flat on your cardboard and draw around—twice. Cut both glasses shapes out. They should be identical.

2. Hold one of the card glasses up to your eyes and mark dots on the lenses that match up to where your pupils are (ask someone to help you get these in the right place). Now line that pair of glasses up with the other pair and use one side of a hole-punch to make a hole where the dot is on each lens. Now you have two identical pairs with eye holes.

3. Dab glue around the edges of the eye holes on one pair of your glasses. Place a few fine white feathers across each hole and hold them in place until they stick. Dab more glue around the lenses and stick the other pair of card glasses down on top, so the holes in both pairs

101 Ways to Become a **Superhero** *... Or an Evil Genius*

match up and the feathers are trapped in between the two sets of lenses.

4. Now you're ready to decorate your X-ray glasses (spirals are popular) and add either some arms, which you can make out of cardboard and stick on, or elastic, so you can wear them like an eye mask.

RATE YOUR GLASSES

Looks | Comfort | Effectiveness

| /10 | /10 | /10 |

Could you see the bones in your hand? [y/n]

Do you have any theories as to how X-ray glasses produce an X-ray effect? [y/n]

If yes, explain below

Did you use this power for....

GOOD? or [ ]

EVIL? [ ]

At the same time you could master these other **Ways**:
5: Super-Vision • **27**: See in the Dark • **43**: Invisibility • **49**: Hone Your Moral Compass • **57**: Photographic Memory • **63**: Observation Skills

Be a Good Influence

Think of someone influential in history. Chances are they weren't the type to sit around complaining when they saw something wasn't right. They probably didn't get famous for criticizing and blaming other people for the wrongs that they saw—they got up and did something about it. Maybe this kind of behavior isn't instinctive for most humans. Maybe that's why when we see someone like that, we're inspired to do the same.

Supermodel

- Assess the influence you have on other people—friends, family, and those you aren't so close to. How well do they listen to you and your ideas? How much are you the focus of conversation and decisions?
- Being a good influence isn't all about persuading people to do things your way: after all, actions speak louder than words. If you see that something needs doing, do it. If someone drops a piece of litter, don't complain and move on—pick it up and put it in the garbage or give it back to them. See how the people around you react.
- To gain influence you need courage to stick your neck out and speak up when others won't. Next time you're with a group of people having a good old grumble about someone, leap to that person's defense. See how quickly others backtrack and try to align with your view.
- Start a new fashion or craze. Begin with something subtle, and when you've proved your fad has followers, go for something more radical (e.g., underwear worn outside pants—or does that give away your identity?).

> **Do as I do . . .** Never say you're going to do something and then not do it. Words must be backed by actions to earn respect. Remember too that sometimes it's better not to say anything, as you may want to keep your head down and blend in with the crowd.

Be a Good Influence **Form**

Once you have mastered this **Way to Become a Superhero**,
stick your Achieved Star here and fill in the form

Achieved

─── YOUR SPHERES OF INFLUENCE ───

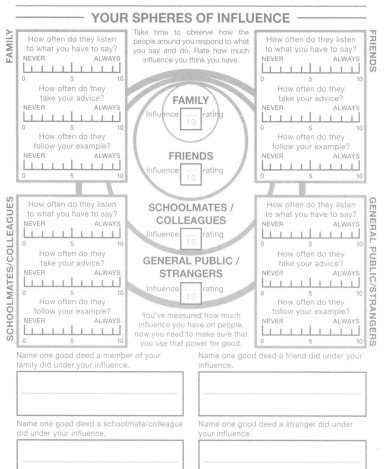

FAMILY

How often do they listen
to what you have to say?
NEVER ___ ALWAYS
|_|_|_|_|_|_|_|_|_|_|
0   5   10

How often do they
take your advice?
NEVER ___ ALWAYS
|_|_|_|_|_|_|_|_|_|_|
0   5   10

How often do they
follow your example?
NEVER ___ ALWAYS
|_|_|_|_|_|_|_|_|_|_|
0   5

Take time to observe how the
people around you respond to what
you say and do. Rate how much
influence you think you have.

FAMILY
Influence [/10] rating

FRIENDS
Influence [/10] rating

**SCHOOLMATES /
COLLEAGUES**
Influence [/10] rating

**GENERAL PUBLIC /
STRANGERS**
Influence [/10] rating

You've measured how much
influence you have on people,
now you need to make sure that
you use that power for good.

FRIENDS

How often do they listen
to what you have to say?
NEVER ___ ALWAYS
|_|_|_|_|_|_|_|_|_|_|
0   5   10

How often do they
take your advice?
NEVER ___ ALWAYS
|_|_|_|_|_|_|_|_|_|_|
0   5   10

How often do they
follow your example?
NEVER ___ ALWAYS
|_|_|_|_|_|_|_|_|_|_|
0   5   10

SCHOOLMATES/COLLEAGUES

How often do they listen
to what you have to say?
NEVER ___ ALWAYS
|_|_|_|_|_|_|_|_|_|_|
0   5   10

How often do they
take your advice?
NEVER ___ ALWAYS
|_|_|_|_|_|_|_|_|_|_|
0   5   10

How often do they
follow your example?
NEVER ___ ALWAYS
|_|_|_|_|_|_|_|_|_|_|
0   5   10

GENERAL PUBLIC/STRANGERS

How often do they listen
to what you have to say?
NEVER ___ ALWAYS
|_|_|_|_|_|_|_|_|_|_|
0   5   10

How often do they
take your advice?
NEVER ___ ALWAYS
|_|_|_|_|_|_|_|_|_|_|
0   5   10

How often do they
follow your example?
NEVER ___ ALWAYS
|_|_|_|_|_|_|_|_|_|_|
0   5   10

Name one good deed a member of your
family did under your influence.

Name one good deed a friend did under your
influence.

Name one good deed a schoolmate/colleague
did under your influence.

Name one good deed a stranger did under
your influence.

At the same time you could master these other **Ways**:
8: Kick Ass Humanely • **35**: Identify Opportunities to Help • **46**: Choose a Cause
93: Develop Powers of Persuasion • **96**: Lead from the Front • **99**: Gather a Superteam

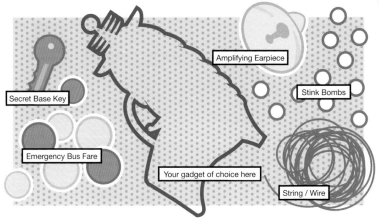

Secret Base Key

Amplifying Earpiece

Stink Bombs

Emergency Bus Fare

Your gadget of choice here

String / Wire

Design Your Own Gadgets

Once you're happy with your identity, it's time to get the kit to fit your specific superhero or evil genius needs. You won't find it all on eBay or at a yard sale, though. You should design the equipment on your wish list and build it to your own specifications to get exactly what you want.

Go Gadget Go!

- Every superhero needs a tool belt: a portable kit of items to help you catch criminals, escape tight spots, and perform special moves. Make a list of gadgets that will assist you with your work (or even supply powers you've been unable to master, such as flight) and that are light and compact. Large devices can be designed for use in your base.
- Think defensive as well as offensive. Think about how to create as well as destroy. Obviously you want lots of flashy technical gear, but gather a mini-pack of basic survival items, like bandages and safety matches too.
- Once your list is final, sketch out designs. Your tools should fit in with the rest of your look and reflect your identity. Give them cool names and remember to incorporate your logo on them somewhere. Make prototypes out of cardboard to get an idea of their look and feel.
- You might not yet have the necessary carpentry, engineering, or metalwork skills to produce a highly finished product, but you may be able to modify an existing gadget to make it into the equipment you want. With some imagination you might be able to transform a piece of old junk into a high-tech piece of ass-kicking gear.

The whole kit and caboodle: If you have a tendency to overpack whenever you go on vacation, you're going to have to learn to be selective. If you're clever you can design gadgets that are multifunctional so that you don't get weighed down by the kitchen sink.

Design Your Own Gadgets **Form**

Once you have mastered this **Way to Become a Superhero**, stick your Achieved Star here and fill in the form

⭐ **Achieved**

BELT UP

It'll be pointless having lots of amazing gadgets if you can't take them all with you on a mission. Make a utility belt out of the mini cereal boxes you get in variety packs. This way you'll be prepared for anything.

WHAT YOU'LL NEED

A variety pack of cereals
Paint
A pair of scissors
A belt

WHAT TO DO

1. Take the first cereal box and eat the contents.

2. Paint the box with a design that matches your outfit.

3. Cut two slits in the back of the box.

4. Thread the belt through the two slits so the box hangs off the front of the belt.

5. Repeat the process with as many cereal boxes as you can fit on your belt.

6. Fill the boxes with your gadgets.

GO GO GIZMO

Name two gadgets you have designed yourself

If other, please specify

Which is your favorite gadget?

What else do you keep in your utility belt?

☐ Fingerprint-dusting kit
☐ Screwdriver
☐ Camera
☐ Recording device
☐ Flashlight
☐ Emergency snacks
☐ Bus fare
☐ First-aid kit
☐ Notepad and pen
☐ Other

Rate the usefulness of your gadgets

⭐ Terrible ⭐ Poor ⭐ Not bad
⭐ Good ⭐ Excellent ⭐ Can't do without them

Did you use this power for...

☐ **GOOD?** or
☐ **EVIL?**

At the same time you could master these other **Ways:**
3: Take Flight • **17**: Choose Your Outfit • **24**: Design a Logo • **32**: Get a Villainous Chair
41: Become a Science Genius • **64**: Travel in Time • **77**: X-Ray Vision

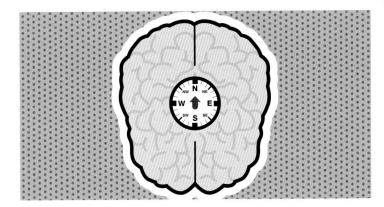

Orientation

It's important not to get caught up in the glamour of being a superhero (or an evil genius). It's all very well to swoop and dive through the air or water, or to run superfast, but you'll end up looking really stupid if at the end of your magnificent display you have no idea where you are, how to get where you're supposed to be going, or even how to get home. Don't let a mission turn into a lost cause because *you* get lost!

Ways and Means

• Things look very different from the air, so before you set out on a mission, check your route on the Internet using an application like Google Earth or look up aerial photographs. This way you can scout out safe places to hide and easy escape routes.
• It's important to know where country borders lie and the names and locations of major cities. Take the test opposite in which you have to identify countries and cities by their landmarks and outlines. Bone up on key geographical data relating to the location of your mission and memorize names and photos that will help you orientate yourself in unknown territories.
• Don't be embarrassed to use a map and compass, but make sure you know how to read them, or you're in real danger of looking like a fool. Join an orienteering club to test your map-reading skills in unknown terrain. If you're really clever you can learn how to read latitude and longitude coordinates to pinpoint locations.

Sun, moon, and stars: They can all help you navigate. For example, the sun rises in the east and sets in the west. If the moon rises before sunset, its illuminated side points roughly west. In the Northern Hemisphere, the bright star above the Plough (Polaris) points north.

Orientation **Form**

Once you have mastered this **Way to Become a Superhero**, stick your Achieved Star here and fill in the form

Achieved

───── WHERE IN THE WORLD AM I? ─────

You don't want to get lost as you fly around the planet on world-saving (or destroying) missions. Learn to recognize important places from unusually high viewpoints, starting with this test . . .

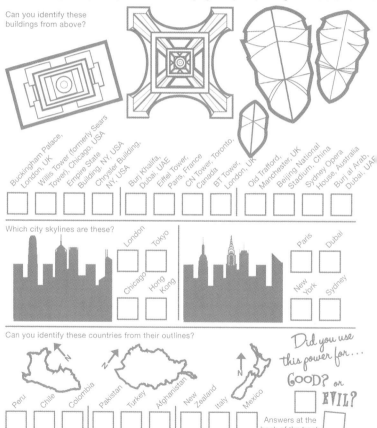

Can you identify these buildings from above?

Buckingham Palace, London, UK
Willis Tower (formerly Sears Tower), Chicago, USA
Empire State Building, NY, USA
Chrysler Building, NY, USA
Burj Khalifa, Dubai, UAE
Eiffel Tower, Paris, France
CN Tower, Toronto, Canada
BT Tower, London, UK
Old Trafford, Manchester, UK
Beijing National Stadium, China
Sydney Opera House, Australia
Burj al Arab, Dubai, UAE

Which city skylines are these?

London
Tokyo
Chicago
Hong Kong

Paris
Dubai
New York
Sydney

Can you identify these countries from their outlines?

Peru
Chile
Colombia
Pakistan
Turkey
Afghanistan
New Zealand
Italy
Mexico

Did you use this power for...

GOOD? or

EVIL?

Answers at the back of the book

At the same time you could master these other **Ways**:
3: Take Flight • **18**: Harness the Elements • **57**: Photographic Memory • **58**: Withstand Heat and Cold • **63**: Observation Skills • **97**: Know What's Happening Everywhere

RESCUE DILEMMA

You've discovered a hostage, a megabomb, and an alien space-ship. Do you . . .

STOP THE TIMER ON THE MEGABOMB

CHASE YOUR NEMESIS ESCAPING WITH HIS ALIEN ALLIES

RESCUE YOUR KIDNAPPED SIDEKICK FROM THE SHARK TANK

GIVE UP AND LEAVE IT TO THE POLICE

Make the Right Decisions—Fast

A superhero is required to make a great many split-second decisions, some of which have life-or-death consequences. If you're a bit of a ditherer, it could be because you like to weigh all the pros and cons, but it's also likely that you lack belief in your own decisions and want someone to approve them or to tell you what to do.

To Do or Not to Do?

- For one day, practice making decisions for someone else, like your sidekick. Every time they are faced with a choice—what to do, when to do it, how to do it—they must consult you and you must decide for them. It's easier when the consequences are limited and it's not you who must face them. But imagine if you were in charge of a group of young children. Then the decisions you make on their behalf are crucial.
- Learn to trust your intuition. For one day, write down each gut feeling you have, from waking up and thinking, "Today is going to be a good day," to having a hunch the sun will come out even though it's cloudy, to knowing what time it is without looking at a clock. Keep a record of your gut feelings and how accurate they turn out to be.
- Making decisions feels harder when the clock is ticking. Give yourself ten seconds to decide 1) what you're going to wear next time you go to a party, 2) what you're going to order next time you're in a restaurant. Did you make good decisions? Would you have chosen differently if you'd had longer? Sometimes having a time limit helps you to focus.

 Make up your mind: Always consider the risks involved in your decision and, where possible, have a backup plan ready. Sometimes there are no right decisions. You have to make the choice that feels best for you, then commit yourself to making it work.

Make the Right Decisions—Fast Form

Once you have mastered this **Way to Become a Superhero**, stick your Achieved Star here and fill in the form

☆ **Achieved**

DECISIONS, DECISIONS

Sometimes it's best to let fate decide. As a last resort, or just for fun, you can use this decision-making spinner to tell you what to do.

WRITE YOUR ANSWER HERE

MAKE A SACRIFICE

SAVE YOURSELF

TRUST YOUR INTUITION

WHATEVER YOU'RE THINKING—DO THE OPPOSITE

THE ANSWER IS "YES"

1. Fill in the missing section of the spinner with another possible answer of your own invention.

2. Photocopy or trace the spinner, glue it to thicker cardboard, and cut it out. Then take a pencil and push it through the center of the spinner.

3. Next time you're faced with a dilemma, ask the spinner your difficult question, then give it a twirl and follow the advice of whichever triangle is directly facing you.

Write your dilemma below, then spin . . .

Did the spinner solve your dilemma? [y/n]

What did fate decide?

Did you use this power for . . .

GOOD? or

☐ **EVIL?** ☐

What action did you take?

At the same time you could master these other **Ways**:
19: Know Whom to Save First • **20**: Learn to Multitask • **29**: Solve Impossible Problems • **53**: Be Ruthless • **70**: Cope Under Pressure • **96**: Lead from the Front

Get a Head for Business

Love of money is the root of all evil, and that's why as an evil genius you should amass stacks of it. If you beg, borrow, or steal to make your fortune you will be missing a trick. A legitimate rise up the ranks of business can help you in many ways: it will lend you respectable cover for your less respectable activities, introduce you to powerful contacts, and provide an education in management and business planning—all of which will come in handy when you're scheming for world domination.

Loaded

- What are you good at and how can you turn that skill into a moneymaking scheme? If you're creative, why not make something to sell, like jewelry, clothes, or cakes? If you're physically fit, consider the sort of jobs you could usefully do for people who can't or don't want to do them themselves, like gardening, decorating, or dog-walking. There might be ways to make money out of nothing—people's unwanted junk.
- Do your research so that the products or services you offer are competitive. Find out how much other people charge.
- Define your market and find ways to reach out to them. You could distribute flyers, set up a website, place an ad in the local paper, or offer discounts. Ask happy customers to give quotable references.
- As you become profitable, make your money work for you. Look for opportunities to expand the business and invest in others, and slowly build your empire. Do plenty of research first to minimize your risks.

> **Savers keepers:** Keep a record of your accounts. You should know exactly how much money you're spending on the business, how much it's earning you and how much profit you're making. Save some money for a rainy day, but any left over is for evil investment.

Get a Head for Business Form

Once you have mastered this **Way to Become an Evil Genius**,
stick your Achieved Star here and fill in the form

☆ Achieved

SAVE FOR THE WORLD

World domination is an expensive business. Start building your funds now by coming up with
some ingenious money-making schemes. Keep track of your earnings here.

Write how you made your
money in the boxes below . . .

Write the amount you
made in the coins . . .

Job 1

Job 2

Job 3

Job 4

Job 5

Job 6

Job 7

Job 8

Job 9

Job 10

Job 11

Job 12

Job 13

How much did you manage
to earn in . . . a week?

$ [0 0] . [0 0]

. . . a month?

$ [0 0 0] . [0 0]

. . . a year?

$ [0 0 0 0] . [0 0]

At the same time you could master these other **Ways**:
23: Plan for World Domination • **32**: Get a Villainous Chair • **33**: Anticipate Your Enemy's
Next Move • **40**: Understand Body Language • **53**: Be Ruthless • **59**: Take Risks

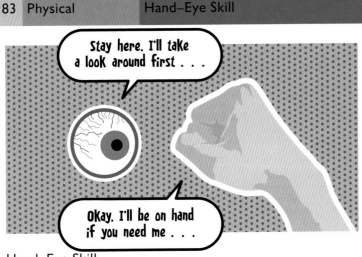

Hand–Eye Skill

Coordinating something as complex as the human body is no mean feat, yet we all do it subconsciously every day. But we had to go through a steep learning curve to get there, from putting that first spoonful of food into our mouth to balancing wooden blocks on top of each other to build a tower. Those tasks now seem simple. Enough of the child's play—it's time for your next steep learning curve.

Brain, Eyes, Action!

- Get yourself warmed up for the challenges that follow by grabbing a needle and some thread. Then get threading. Have a competition with your sidekick to see who can thread a needle first. If you get a taste for needlework, include embroidery in your training program.
- Take two tennis balls and draw "1" on one and "2" on the other. Ask your sidekick to throw both to you at once, calling out "1" or "2" as they do so. You must catch the right one. Any type of catching game is good practice. In fact, almost any sport will improve your hand–eye skills, but for some really intense training, try archery or Ping-Pong.
- Playing video games may not be the most intellectually edifying way of practicing hand–eye coordination, but it is one of the most fun.
- Processing pages of little black dots into the movement of fingers on an instrument requires study, practice, and lots of hand–eye skill, but the rewards of being able to read and play music make it worth the effort.

Drawing to a conclusion: When we're little we're often asked to trace shapes, as this is a great way to develop hand–eye skill. Now you should be beyond that. Practice drawing what you see—a still life, a landscape, a human model—and try to nail every last detail.

Hand–Eye Skill **Form**

Once you have mastered this **Way to Become a Superhero**,
stick your Achieved Star here and fill in the form

Achieved

─── **FROM HERE TO THE MOON** ───

Hand-eye coordination is essential in many professions. This test is based on an actual coordination test for astronauts.

The object of the mission is to draw a single continuous line from the center of the Earth to the center of the Moon as quickly as possible WITHOUT going over the lines.

THINGS YOU'LL NEED

1. A photocopier (or scanner and printer)
2. Tape
3. Two different colored pens
4. Your sidekick
5. A stopwatch
6. A shopping bag
7. A 2 lb weight

WHAT TO DO

1. Photocopy or scan this page, making sure you enlarge the image by 100%. Print out at least three sheets and tape the first one to the wall at eye level.

2. Stand at arm's length from the sheet and, holding one of the pens, place the point at the center of the Earth.

3. Your sidekick should count you down from three and start the timer as you begin the test. Shout out when you get to the finish circle on the Moon to tell your sidekick to stop the timer.

4. Now try the test again with a new printout, but this time hang the shopping bag with the 2 lb weight in it from your arm.

5. Try the test a third time without the weight again. Your arm will probably feel light and floaty now. After each attempt, let your sidekick have a try using the other colored pen and compare skill levels.

RATE YOUR SUCCESS

Attempt 1   /10

Attempt 2   /10

Attempt 3   /10

Did you use this power for...
GOOD? or
☐ **EVIL?**
☐

At the same time you could master these other **Ways**:
20: Learn to Multitask • **21**: Dexterity • **24**: Design a Logo • **28**: Balance • **66**: Agility
79: Design Your Own Gadgets • **94**: Talk to Computers

WARNING: DO NOT PRESS THIS BUTTON

Resist Temptation

There are some temptations one need have no qualms about surrendering to, like, "Hmm, I'd really like to cook a meal for my friends," or "It'd be great to spend a day helping at the old people's home." If you do experience qualms about such things, go to the Supervillainous section. As a superhero you need to worry about things that you cannot resist even though they're bad for you. Your enemies will be quick to exploit such weaknesses.

Qualm Down!

- Start by making a list of everyday temptations that you know are bad but that you frequently succumb to, like watching TV instead of helping the person slaving over a hot stove to make your dinner, or cracking a joke at someone else's expense to make your friends laugh even though you know it might hurt their feelings.
- The list you've made is essentially one of negative actions. The way to fight them is to counter them with positive actions—not ones that provide a dull or unpleasant antidote, but ones you can thrive on and even enjoy. Add a second column to your list and come up with inspiring positive actions to put into practice the next time you're tempted.
- As a superhero, you'll need to resist the temptation to press that big red button, to tell someone you love who you really are, to use your powers for selfish purposes, or to let your rage boil over and make you do something that makes you as bad as your nemesis. Start reminding yourself now of all the reasons why these are very bad ideas.

Negative charge: Resisting temptation can be as much about what you do as what you don't do. Laziness, fear, selfishness—don't let these negative vibes nip a positive action in the bud. Your qualms should tell you when doing nothing is not the thing to do.

Resist Temptation **Form**

Once you have mastered this **Way to Become a Superhero**,
stick your Achieved Star here and fill in the form

Achieved

--- **NEGATIVE VS. POSITIVE** ---

Below you'll find examples of some common superhero temptations. Put your powers of
resistance into practice by coming up with positive actions to counter the negative ones. Be
honest about which option you went for when you encountered these temptations.

TEMPTATION	–IVE ACTION	+IVE ACTION	YOUR CHOICE
You find the last piece of cake left in your secret base	Eat it before your sidekick shows up		
You see your call signal beaming into the sky but your favorite TV show has just started	Close the curtains and pump up the volume		
You find your girl/boyfriend's diary. They've been asking you a lot of probing questions lately . . .	Read it from cover to cover		
You've just handed your nemesis over to the cops when you come across his or her vast stash of cash	Head off to the mall for some serious retail therapy		
Your nemesis offers you a 50:50 share of the power if you join him or her in taking over the world	Say, "Where do I sign?"		
Write your own dilemma here			

At the same time you could master these other **Ways**:
1: Discover Your Alter Ego • **26**: Know Your Weaknesses • **35**: Identify Opportunities to
Help • **44**: Never Give Up • **81**: Make the Right Decisions—Fast • **86**: Keep Supersecrets

Shape-Shift

Everyone has the ability to change their appearance in one way or another, even if it isn't possible to physically mutate into different organisms. But that doesn't mean you won't ever acquire this special power: if you work hard at science, maybe you can come up with the genetic solution to controlled mutation. Or perhaps you'll just get lucky and fall into a vat of radioactive goo that will give you the power. More likely, you'll have to start at the bottom and transform the old-fashioned way.

Transformers

- It's generally accepted that to shape-shift successfully it's important first to learn how to do this mentally, probing into your subject's consciousness and seeing through their eyes. The physical transformation will then follow. So pick a subject to practice on. Don't run before you can walk—go for a basic organism like a slug, as it'll be easier to enter its uncomplex mind. Then you could move on to a sheep and so on. Finally, try it on a human: someone you know well but who has no idea you might be trying to enter their mind and meld it with your own.
- Impersonation is a form of shape-shifting. You need to study your subject intently, from what they look like, to the way they move, the pitch and tone of their voice, their gestures—even their handwriting. Start with an easy subject—someone you vaguely resemble and who has easily identifiable mannerisms. Practice in a mirror and record your own voice to assess how well you're doing. Take some acting classes.

 Get in on the act: There's a technique you can try called "the Method," which some actors use to become a character. They draw on their own memories and experiences to bring depth to the role. Sometimes they live in this role even when they're offstage or off camera.

Shape-Shift **Form**

Once you have mastered this **Way to Become a Superhero**, stick your Achieved Star here and fill in the form

☆ **Achieved**

———— SHAPE UP OR SHIP OUT ————

Hosting a costume party is the perfect way to try out your shape-shifting powers. No one will think you're odd if you don't quite pull it off and, as everyone there will know you, it'll be the ultimate test of your powers' effectiveness. Fool your friends and you can fool anyone. Perform three shape-shifts during the party, slipping away to transform in secret. This will put people off your scent.

—— MORPH INTO A FAMOUS PERSON . . . ——

Whom did you morph into?

Place a photo of yourself as this person here

Rate your shape-shifting powers:

Appearance ☐/10 Voice ☐/10 Mannerisms ☐/10 Overall ☐/10

How many people guessed it was really you?

No one ☐   A few ☐   A lot ☐   Everyone ☐

———— AN ANIMAL . . . ————

Place a photo of yourself as this animal here

What did you morph into?

Rate your shape-shifting powers:

Appearance ☐/10 Voice ☐/10 Behavior ☐/10 Overall ☐/10

How many people guessed it was really you?

No one ☐   A few ☐   A lot ☐   Everyone ☐

— ANOTHER PARTY GUEST . . . —

Whom did you morph into?

Rate your shape-shifting powers:

Appearance ☐/10 Voice ☐/10

Mannerisms ☐/10 Overall ☐/10

How many people guessed it was really you?

No one ☐   A few ☐   A lot ☐   Everyone ☐

Place a photo of yourself as this person here

Did you use this power for . . . **GOOD?** ☐ or **EVIL?** ☐

At the same time you could master these other **Ways**:
12: Mind Control • **22**: Communicate with Animals • **40**: Understand Body Language
47: Master of Illusion • **63**: Observation Skills • **92**: Telepathy

Keep Supersecrets

The public and media are a fickle bunch. You can be their savior one day and their whipping boy the next. This is another reason why anonymity is vital. Protecting the secret of your identity will require you to lie, bluff, let people down, and sometimes act like a complete weirdo. But that's the price of being a superhero.

Keeping the Cat in the Bag

- If you can learn to keep other people's secrets you have a better chance of keeping your own, so forbid yourself from gossiping. If you gain a reputation for being able to keep secrets well, you'll also benefit from it, as you'll be better informed as to what people are up to.
- When you overhear people talking about your superhero alter ego, join in, even if they're being nasty. This is method acting. You have to convince yourself you don't know who this superhero dude is. At all costs resist the temptation to take credit for your amazing deeds.
- Prepare and rehearse watertight cover stories to explain any odd behavior you may exhibit because of your secret double life, so that when it comes to using them, you can lie convincingly.
- Encrypt your secret files and protect them with uncrackable passwords.
- Unburden yourself on your trusted sidekick. Alternatively, every now and then, go somewhere you are guaranteed to be completely alone and shout your secrets to the wind. Or write them down on a piece of paper, then destroy it. You'll feel so much better.

 Bare-faced liar: If someone gets a whiff of your secret life, don't overexplain or get defensive. Acting like you've got something to hide will only make them more eager to extract your secrets. Try to relax, look them in the eye, and lie. Don't feel bad. It's the only way.

Keep Supersecrets **Form**

Once you have mastered this **Way to Become a Superhero**,
stick your Achieved Star here and fill in the form

Achieved

— SECRET IDENTITY —

Keeping a secret as huge as a double life is no mean feat. It's inevitable that you'll be asked
some pretty awkward questions from time to time, so you should prepare a set of excuses to
cover your tracks.

QUESTION 1

Where do you keep
disappearing off to?

EXCUSE 1

QUESTION 4

How do you know so
much about (write local
incident here)?

EXCUSE 4

QUESTION 2

How did you get here so
incredibly fast?

EXCUSE 2

QUESTION 5

Why is your
underwear on the outside
of your pants?

EXCUSE 5

QUESTION 3

You said you had to
leave early yesterday to get
to bed early, so why
are you so tired?

EXCUSE 3

Do you think people
believed your excuses?

EXCUSE 1 [y/n]

EXCUSE 2 [y/n]

EXCUSE 3 [y/n]

EXCUSE 4 [y/n]

EXCUSE 5 [y/n]

Did you use
this power for...
GOOD? or
[ ] EVIL?
[ ]

At the same time you could master these other **Ways**:
9: Select a Sidekick • **40**: Understand Body Language • **65**: Talk Your Way
Out of Trouble • **84**: Resist Temptation • **89**: Know When Someone's Lying

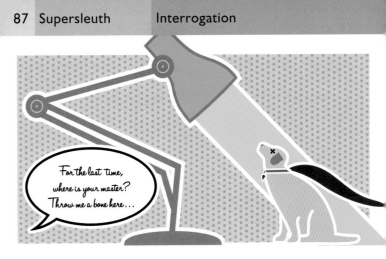

Interrogation

Some people will bend over backward to help you catch the bad guys; others will need more encouragement. There are lots of reasons a person might have for clamming up—fear of the repercussions, the desire to protect someone, stalling for time. Asking the right questions and being able to read the answers (both spoken and in body language) takes practice.

Tough Talking

- Choosing an interrogation technique will depend very much on whom you're interrogating and how desperate the situation is. Whatever you do, try to remain in control. Acting enraged is fine as long as you're a sea of calm underneath. Evil geniuses will explore all your weaknesses in a bid to claim back power, so don't let them get under your skin.
- Start with some casual conversation in order to establish a good rapport with your interviewee. This will put them at ease and make them talk more freely. Ask them to describe events in detail and take notes. Then ask them similar questions again to check for inconsistencies.
- Role-play interrogation scenarios with your sidekick. Imagine you've apprehended your nemesis, and you need them to tell you where they've planted their bomb before it goes off. Then swap places and pretend you've been caught in a trap by your enemy and are being pressed to reveal the whereabouts of your secret base. You should also play out interrogation scenes with your nemesis's love interest and with one of their associates.

Ways of making you talk: Supervillains aren't known for their patience and tend to opt for torture as an interrogation method. Prepare yourself both mentally and physically for this—tactics are important. Do or say whatever is necessary to increase your chances of escape.

Interrogation Form

Once you have mastered this **Way to Become a Superhero**, stick your Achieved Star here and fill in the form

Achieved

——— UNQUESTIONABLE ———

Ask your sidekick to take part in some interrogation role plays. You'll only benefit from them if you both immerse yourselves in the roles and try to simulate accurately how you and your nemesis would react in the imaginary situations below. Let the power game commence . . .

ROLE PLAY 1: INTERVIEWER

You've caught your nemesis red-handed. You know he or she has planted a bomb but you don't know where. Try to extract this information, or at least get some clues.

What was your opening question/remark?

What question/remark got the most helpful response from the interviewee?

Did you control your temper? [y/n] If no, what made you lose control?

Did they give you the info you were after? [y/n]

Did your tactics include . . .

. . . confrontation? [y/n] . . . ego-stroking? [y/n]

. . . deception? [y/n] . . . intimidation? [y/n]

. . . cooperation (i.e., exchange of info)? [y/n]

Overall, where did the balance of power lie?

You [ ] Your interviewee [ ]

ROLE PLAY 2: INTERVIEWEE

You've been captured by your nemesis. He or she wants the location of your secret base in order to steal your gadgets and files. Can you endure their interrogation and find a way to escape?

How did you respond to their questions?

With stony silence [ ] With lies [ ]

With more questions [ ] With laughter [ ]

With insults [ ] With tears [ ]

Did your interviewer . . .

. . . threaten you? [y/n] . . . sweet-talk you? [y/n]

. . . humiliate you? [y/n] . . . trick you? [y/n]

. . . offer you a deal? [y/n] . . . torture you? [y/n]

Did you reveal the information they were after? [y/n]

If no, how close did you get to crumbling?

Nowhere near [ ]

Quite close [ ]

Very close [ ]

Did you use this power for . . . GOOD? or EVIL?

Overall, where did the balance of power lie?

You [ ] Your interviewee [ ]

At the same time you could master these other **Ways**:
6: Stamina • **65**: Talk Your Way Out of Trouble • **70**: Cope Under Pressure
72: Speak a Hundred Languages • **89**: Know When Someone's Lying • **92**: Telepathy

Acquire Specialist Knowledge

If you thought being a superhero was all about carrying out spectacular physical feats, think again. You also need to be an all-around genius. No amount of knowledge is too much, nor will it ever be enough. It takes brains (and evil) to become an evil genius, and if you're to stand any chance against one, you need to be able to match their mental mastery.

Brawny Brains

- Each year, pick a highly specialist topic that you would like to become an expert in. Research everything you can about that subject and aim to write a book (or thesis, at least) at the end of your research.

- Select topics no one else has ever become expert in before and that you think will have some useful application in your superhero/villain career. There's a book called *Lightweight Sandwich Construction*—such expertise may be of some day-to-day use, but not for superbeings. On the other hand, a book called *The Benefit of Farting* might well have been written by a superhero or villain with the vision to see all sorts of hitherto unknown but tactical uses for flatulence. These subjects already have their experts though—you must come up with your own.

- In order to be able to forge relationships with people and gain their trust, it's useful to find some common ground. You should be able to engage in a little conversation on a variety of topics, such as sports, television, weather, and current affairs. Start watching game shows and pitting yourself against the contestants. Can you beat their scores?

Culture vulture: Science and engineering expertise comes in handy in life-or-death situations, but don't underestimate the power of words, music, and art: in the wrong hands they can become lethal weapons, but they can also empower and liberate people.

Acquire Specialist Knowledge **Form**

Once you have mastered this **Way to Become a Superhero**, stick your Achieved Star here and fill in the form

Achieved

— KNOW-IT-ALL —

Complete this diploma certificate when you have become the master of your specialist subject.

THE 101 SUPERHERO ACADEMY OF EXCELLENCE PROUDLY AWARDS A DIPLOMA TO

> Your name here

IN RECOGNITION OF SUPERHUMAN KNOWLEDGE IN THE FIELD OF

> Your specialist subject here

What have you discovered that no one else knows?

How do you plan to apply this knowledge in your superhuman career?

Rate your level of expertise in this subject

Disappointing (Third Class)

Satisfactory (Second Class – 2:2)

Good (Second Class – 2:1)

Excellent (First Class)

Did you use this power for...

GOOD? or

☐ *EVIL?*

☐

At the same time you could master these other **Ways**:
22: Communicate with Animals • **40**: Understand Body Language • **41**: Become a Science Genius • **72**: Speak a Hundred Languages • **94**: Talk to Computers

Know When Someone's Lying

Superheroes and villains can't afford to be too trusting. People lie for all kinds of reasons, but it's usually to protect themselves or someone else. In your profession you will find yourself surrounded by people who need to protect themselves, so it's vital for you to tell truth from fiction.

Don't Sweat It

- When people lie they tend to avoid direct eye contact, sometimes by blinking a lot, and they often fidget or cough. Their heartbeat increases, so they might breathe more heavily or look flushed. They have a tendency to compensate for their lies by over-explaining or giving information with too much detail. Look for these signs.
- Set people up so that you can observe their behavior when lying. For example, you could get your sidekick to take a friend out shopping for your birthday present and then quiz them about where they've been when they get back. Or you could leave an irresistible piece of chocolate or some cash lying in the way of someone as bait.
- Ask your sidekick some probing personal questions that you think they may be unwilling to be completely honest about. Don't tell them it's a lie-detector test until the end, when you reveal your conclusions. They can confirm or deny any lies without telling you the true answers, if they wish.
- Reverse the test so that you become the subject. Learning how to spot a liar will make you more proficient at lying yourself, and this can be just as valuable a skill for superheroes and villains alike.

Eye spy: Very accomplished liars will have no problem looking you directly in the eye when they lie. But examine their eyes carefully. Is there emotion in them to back up the claims coming from the mouth? Their eyes may be saying something very different.

Know When Someone's Lying **Form**

Once you have mastered this **Way to Become a Superhero,**
stick your Achieved Star here and fill in the form

Achieved

PANTS ON FIRE

Come up with three personal questions to ask your sidekick and see if you can detect whether
they're lying or not. Tell them it is a test, but don't tell them what sort of test. Record their answers
and any behavior you observe that suggests they're not being entirely honest.

Question 1	Their answer	Any signs of lying

Do you suspect them of lying? [y/n]   Did you probe them for more information? [y/n]   Did they admit to lying? (Don't confront them till the end of the test.) [y/n]

Question 2	Their answer	Any signs of lying

Do you suspect them of lying? [y/n]   Did you probe them for more information? [y/n]   Did they admit to lying? (Don't confront them till the end of the test.) [y/n]

Question 3	Their answer	Any signs of lying

Do you suspect them of lying? [y/n]   Did you probe them for more information? [y/n]   Did they admit to lying? (Don't confront them till the end of the test.) [y/n]

YOU LIAR

Being able to lie convincingly is a useful skill. Reverse the test so your sidekick becomes the interviewer. Lie through your teeth and see if you can get away with it.

If you were caught, what gave you away?

Lots of blinking [y/n]   Inconsistency in your answer [y/n]

Fidgeting [y/n]   Giving more info than you needed [y/n]

How many lies did you get away with? [3]

Looking nervous [y/n]   Lack of eye contact [y/n]

Did you use this power for...

GOOD? or [ ]

EVIL? [ ]

At the same time you could master these other **Ways:**
33: Anticipate Your Enemy's Next Move • **40**: Understand Body Language
63: Observation Skills • **74**: Identify and Interpret Clues • **92**: Telepathy

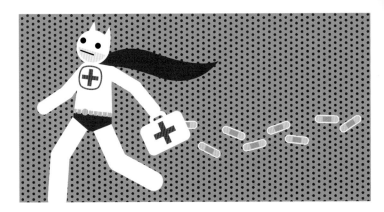

Healing

Ordinary people can unexpectedly become heroes when they act quickly in an emergency and save someone's life. As a superhero, this must be your daily business. The world is your operating room—it's time to scrub up.

All's Well That Mends Well

- Take a first-aid course. If you don't know how to help someone who can't breathe, who's choking or bleeding, you're never going to nail this healing thing. Other key skills you should learn are: how to clean and dress wounds; what to do if someone's been electrocuted or poisoned; how to treat burns, bites, and stings; and how to perform CPR.
- For centuries herbs and plants have been used as remedies for all sorts of ailments. Everyone knows about aloe plants, but were you aware, for example, that lavender has antiseptic, antibacterial, and even antibiotic properties? You can use the flowers to make tea for drinking or for anointing wounds. The smell is soothing and relaxing—except to moths (so if you're attacked by giant mothmen, you'll know what to do). However, like other medicines, herbs can be extremely potent and harmful if used wrongly, so you really need to know your stuff.
- There are lots of other alternative types of medicine that you could explore and that might suit your superpowers well. For example, if you were a specialist in force fields, you may well discover you have the power to heal people using a type of magnet therapy or therapeutic touch. Or if mind control is your strong point, try hypnotherapy.

Dead cert: Even you can't bring the dead back to life. A person may be resuscitated some time after "clinical death" (when the heart stops beating) but the risk of brain damage is high after just three minutes—longer if the victim's body temperature is lower than normal.

Healing Form

Once you have mastered this **Way to Become a Superhero**, stick your Achieved Star here and fill in the form

Achieved

————————SUPER-AID QUIZ————————

You should call 911 in the event of any genuine first-aid emergency. However, there may be things you can do for the victim before medical help arrives. Test your first-aid knowledge with this quiz. There is only one correct answer for each question. The other actions could be ineffective or even dangerous.

1. Your victim is suffering from heatstroke. Do you . . .

a. . . . give them a hug and say, "Hang in there"?
b. . . . give them lots of water and wrap them in a cold wet sheet?
c. . . . give them a cup of tea and wrap them in a warm blanket?
d. . . . give them mouth-to-mouth resuscitation?

2. Your victim has been scalded by boiling water. Do you . . .

a. . . . run cold water over the burn for ten minutes, then wrap it in plastic wrap to keep it clean?
b. . . . run cold water over the burn for five minutes, then wrap it in clean towels?
c. . . . apply antiseptic cream and put a bandage on it?
d. . . . rub olive oil on the burn?

3. Your victim is choking on something. They've tried coughing it up but it hasn't worked. Do you . . .

a. . . . turn them upside down and give them a shake?
b. . . . give them a drink of water?
c. . . . look down their throat and try to remove the obstruction?
d. . . . administer up to five blows with the heel of your hand between their shoulder blades?

4. You arrive at the scene of a disaster with many victims. Having checked first for danger, you go to their aid. Whom do you help first?

a. The victim who is lying quietly on their back with their eyes closed
b. The victim who is moaning and obviously in great pain
c. The victim who is screaming hysterically
d. The victim who is bleeding heavily from a leg wound

5. Your victim has been electrocuted. Do you . . .

a. . . . give them a shake to see if they're all right?
b. . . . pull the electrical device out of their hands?
c. . . . disconnect them from the power source by turning the current off at the source?
d. . . . throw water over them?

6. Your victim is suffering from hypothermia. Do you . . .

a. . . . give them a shot of brandy?
b. . . . get them out of any wet clothes and wrap them in warm blankets?
c. . . . make them run around to warm them up?
d. . . . run them a hot bath and put them in it?

7. Your victim has been stung by an insect. Do you . . .

a. . . . pull the sting out with a pair of tweezers?
b. . . . suck the sting out?
c. . . . scrape the sting away with the blunt edge of a knife?
d. . . . put a bandage over the sting?

8. Your victim is suffering from persistent central chest pains and breathlessness. You've checked their pulse and it is weak and irregular. What is the likely cause?

a. Food poisoning
b. Heart attack
c. Concussion
d. Stroke

Answers at the back of the book

DISCLAIMER: The content provided in this **Way to Become a Superhero** is for general information only. It should not substitute for the medical advice of your own doctor or any other healthcare professional. The authors are not responsible or liable for any diagnosis made by a reader based on this content.

Did you use this power for . . .
GOOD? or
☐ EVIL?
☐

At the same time you could master these other **Ways**:
13: Conquer Your Fears • **35:** Identify Opportunities to Help • **70:** Cope Under Pressure • **77:** X-Ray Vision • **83:** Hand–Eye Skill • **88:** Acquire Specialist Knowledge

Design Your Supertransport

As fleet-footed as you may be, sometimes you need to get somewhere faster than even superhuman speed can take you. You may also need transport for protection, for carrying equipment, or just to look cool. If you don't drive, your options will be limited, but don't be downhearted. We all have to start somewhere. Besides, a man-powered vehicle is much more eco-friendly. Gas is so last century!

On Your Bike!

- Now, it may take some years before you have the engineering know-how or the money to build an invisible jet or a car to rival the Batmobile, but that doesn't mean you can't start working on a design. Get going on some detailed sketches of your supertransport, inside and out, with labels to show what sort of gadgets you will incorporate.
- Once you're satisfied with your design, try building a prototype out of whatever materials you have available. Old cardboard boxes would be a good start, and make sure you let the creative juices flow.
- While your final superhero vehicle is a work in progress, you can make do by adapting some form of transport you already have, like a skateboard, a bike, a pogo stick, a sled, or a go-cart. The hard work has already been done for you. All you need to do is add some special superhero features—like a laser, a guidance system, a tractor beam, some extra armor and camouflage—and make sure your transport is branded and has the look to go with your outfit and message.

 Home, James: Autopilot is a great feature to have if you can afford it, but you may need to rely on maps or GPS to get you to your destination to begin with. Invest in antitheft devices, though. You won't be able to keep an eye on your supertransport all the time.

Design Your Supertransport **Form**

Once you have mastered this **Way to Become a Superhero**, stick your Achieved Star here and fill in the form

Achieved

──────── SUPERSPEEDY ────────

If you don't have the funds or engineering expertise to invest in a flashy supercar, sub, or plane yet, be creative with what you've got. Make your ride, be it a bike or scooter, truly super with some clever add-ons and slick design.

What is your supertransport vehicle?

☐ Pogo stick ☐ Sled ☐ Go-cart ☐ Bicycle ☐ Skateboard ☐ Other

If other, please specify

_____

How did you make your ride super? With . . .

☐ . . . my superlogo ☐ . . . superarmor ☐ . . . a super-sound system ☐ . . . flame decorations ☐ . . . superweapons ☐ Other

If other, please specify

Not only do you want your super-transport to look awesome, you'll need it to be super-fast. Mark on the speedometer here how fast you were able to go on your supertransport of choice.

30 35 Faster...
25
20
15
10
5
0
kph
mph

Rate your supertransport for performance in the following areas:

Looks ☐ /10

Speed ☐ /10

Security ☐ /10

Special features ☐ /10

Place a photo of your supertransport before its makeover here

Place a photo of your supertransport after its makeover here

Did you use this power for...
GOOD? or
☐ **EVIL?**

At the same time you could master these other **Ways**:
3: Take Flight • 39: Speed • 64: Travel in Time • 76: Devise an Escape Plan
79: Design Your Own Gadgets • 94: Talk to Computers

Telepathy

You're probably thinking: *Reading minds—what a load of garbage!* Well, are you? If you are, this just goes to show that anyone can take a crack at elementary mind-reading. However, like all the skills in this book, it's not elementary level we're aiming at here, it's superlevel. It's knowing your enemy is sneaking up behind you, or about to push the alarm button under his desk, or preparing to escape through a secret trapdoor below him . . .

Give Me a Piece of Your Mind

- Start with a simple bit of number reading. Ask a friend to think of a number between one and ten. Tell them to double it, add six, divide by two, and take away the number they first thought of. You know already (don't you?) that the answer will be . . . three. Do this a few times, changing the number they add to two, four, eight, or ten, and each time you'll mysteriously know that the number they first thought of was half the amount of the number you asked them to add.
- Prepare a set of cards with different symbols drawn on them (e.g., a triangle, a star, a diamond, etc.). Ask your sidekick to test your powers by sitting opposite you with the pile of cards on the table between you. They should pick up one card, carefully hiding it from you, and concentrate on the image on that card. Now relax, empty your mind of other thoughts, and try to tune in to their mind. Your sidekick should start by alternating between just three cards, but as your telepathy skills improve, he or she can add more to make the task more difficult.

 Predict this . . . Conduct a "thought" interview. Ask a friend (and later, when you're more skilled, a stranger) a set of questions and as they write down their answers, scribble down your predictions. Afterward, compare to see how accurate you were.

Telepathy **Form**

Once you have mastered this **Way to Become a Superhero**, stick your Achieved Star here and fill in the form

Achieved

——— I KNEW YOU'D SAY THAT ———

Your sidekick can help you to develop your psychic abilities. Sit opposite each other at a table and ask them to picture the following things in their mind, concentrating on them for ten seconds while you draw the image you receive from them. Don't let them see what you're doing, but at the end of the test check to see how accurate your readings were. Ask your sidekick to think . . .

. . . of a shape. Draw that shape in the space below.

How close were you?
☐ Spot on ☐ Pretty close ☐ Way off

. . . of an animal. Draw that animal in the space below.

How close were you?
☐ Spot on ☐ Pretty close ☐ Way off

. . . of a number between 1 and 100. Write that number in the space below.

How close were you?
☐ Spot on ☐ Pretty close ☐ Way off

. . . of a color. Write the name of that color in the space below.

How close were you?
☐ Spot on ☐ Pretty close ☐ Way off

. . . of someone. Draw the face of that person in the space below. You could try their name too.

How close were you?
☐ Spot on ☐ Pretty close ☐ Way off

. . . of a letter. Write that letter in the space below.

How close were you?
☐ Spot on ☐ Pretty close ☐ Way off

. . . of any object they like. Draw that object in the space below.

How close were you?
☐ Spot on ☐ Pretty close ☐ Way off

. . . of a sequence of five numbers. Write that sequence in the space below.

0 , 0 , 0 , 0 , 0

How many numbers did you get right? ☐ 0   How many of those did you get in the right order? ☐ 0

How close were you?
☐ Spot on ☐ Pretty close ☐ Way off

Rate your telepathic skills: 10

Did you use this power for . . .

GOOD? or EVIL? ☐

At the same time you could master these other **Ways**:
12: Mind Control • **40**: Understand Body Language • **50**: Second Sight
52: Telekinesis

Oh go on...
Just do it for me

Please?
Pretty please?

It'll be in your
best interests...

This is your
last chance...

Develop Powers of Persuasion

In your role as superhero you may be called upon to use your brute strength, your awesome speed, and your nerves of steel. But if you have a way with words, you can try to avoid really nasty situations altogether. You might need to persuade someone not to do a terrible thing (like jump off a tall building, or push the "detonate" button on a bomb) or else persuade someone they can do something they don't feel brave enough to try.

Golden Touch, Silver Tongue

- If someone's really determined to do (or not do) something, you should listen to them to try to understand the sort of person they are and the sort of approach they might respond to. Try to see things from their point of view—that way you'll be able to anticipate their arguments.
- Set an example. One of the best ways to persuade people there's a better way is to show them that better way. When you need people not to panic, it won't help to run around screaming "Don't panic!!!" at them.
- Start off your training with simple tasks, like persuading a friend to share their lunch with you or give you their last piece of chocolate. Gradually you can move on to harder things. See if you can get someone to give you something they really, really love. This will be easier if that someone is a friend, but what about someone you hardly know? Could you persuade them to give you the clothes off their back?
- You can practice when you're out shopping. See if you can haggle successfully, persuading someone to sell you something at a discount.

Whatever you do, don't press the red button: It's amazing how putting pressure on someone to do or not do something will often make them want to do the very opposite. Reverse psychology is one of the sneakier persuasion techniques you can try.

Develop Powers of Persuasion **Form**

Once you have mastered this **Way to Become a Superhero**, stick your Achieved Star here and fill in the form

☆ **Achieved**

─────── PERSUADE SOMEONE . . . ───────

. . . TO DONATE MONEY TO YOUR "SECRET PROJECT" Did it work? [y/n]

If yes, whom did you persuade?

[ ]

How much money did you get? $ [0 , 0] . [0 , 0]

How did you persuade them?

[ ]

. . . TO DO YOUR DIRTY WORK FOR YOU Did it work? [y/n]

If yes, whom did you persuade?

[ ]

What did you persuade them to do?

[ ]

How did you persuade them?

[ ]

. . . TO DO SOMETHING THEY'RE SCARED OF DOING Did it work? [y/n]

If yes, whom did you persuade?

[ ]

What did you persuade them to do?

[ ]

How did you persuade them?

[ ]

. . . NOT TO DO SOMETHING GOOD/BAD* (*DELETE AS APPROPRIATE) Did it work? [y/n]

If yes, whom did you persuade?

[ ]

What did you persuade them not to do?

[ ]

How did you persuade them?

[ ]

What's the hardest thing you've ever had to persuade someone to do?

[ ]

What's your preferred persuasion technique?

Reason with them [ ]   Beg them [ ]

Bribe them [ ]   Threaten them [ ]

Rate your powers of persuasion

☆ Awful   ☆ Poor   ☆ Average

☆ Good   ☆ Very good   ☆ Excellent

Did you use this power for . . . .
GOOD? or
[ ] **EVIL?**
[ ]

At the same time you could master these other **Ways**:
40: Understand Body Language • **78**: Be a Good Influence • **92**: Telepathy
96: Lead from the Front

Talk to Computers

There's no room for technophobes in the pantheon of superheroes. If you are afraid of apps, are suspicious of servers, and dread databases, it's time to face those fears and learn to make computers your friends. You'll need them to access your enemies' secret files, break door codes, and defuse devices.

Save and Quit

- Computer jargon can be intimidating. Begin by teaching yourself some of the basic terminology (like megabyte, install, optimize, configure) and try dropping these words into conversation so that they become familiar.
- The next step is to master day-to-day electronic devices, such as your calculator, microwave, and TV. You may think you already have this one in the bag, but do you really know what all those buttons do? Learn how to use every single one—it is valuable training for interfacing with more complex technology. You might even discover some handy functions.
- Think like a computer. It's the only way to get into their processors. A computer does not allow emotions to influence its operations. It doesn't go the scenic route because it's pretty. It works out the path of least resistance and takes it. Next time someone asks you for your opinion on something, answer as a computer would—rational, unbiased, clinical.
- Visual Basic is one of the easier programming languages you can teach yourself, with the help of a manual, or C, or C++. Get geeky.
- Learn some HTML (also very easy) and create a simple website. If you can learn Flash you'll be able to do flashier things online.

Escape: When it's all going to hell, and that countdown clock keeps ticking down, press the Escape key or try Control, Alt + Delete on a PC (Command + Z on a Mac). Failing that, find the power supply and switch it off: a simple but much overlooked way to save humanity.

Talk to Computers **Form**

Once you have mastered this **Way to Become a Superhero**,
stick your Achieved Star here and fill in the form

Achieved

———————— UPGRADE ————————

As part of your superhuman apprenticeship you need to take your technological expertise to
new levels. It's not enough to know where the on/off buttons are. This week teach yourself how
to do something new with the technology lying around at home.

TV	TELEPHONE/CELL	MICROWAVE

What new function did you
learn to use?

What new function did you
learn to use?

What new function did you
learn to use?

How useful will it be?
Rate it out of ten | 10 |

How useful will it be?
Rate it out of ten | 10 |

How useful will it be?
Rate it out of ten | 10 |

Did you have to refer to
the instructions? | y/n |

Did you have to refer to
the instructions? | y/n |

Did you have to refer to
the instructions? | y/n |

WASHING MACHINE	COMPUTER	

How good are you with
technology? Rate yourself out
of ten in the following areas:

Confidence | 10 | Patience | 10 | Problem-solving | 10 | Speed | 10 |

What new function did you
learn to use?

What new function did you
learn to use?

*Did you use
this power for....*

GOOD? or

☐ **EVIL?**

☐

How useful will it be?
Rate it out of ten | 10 |

How useful will it be?
Rate it out of ten | 10 |

Did you have to refer to
the instructions? | y/n |

Did you have to refer to
the instructions? | y/n |

At the same time you could master these other **Ways**:
15: Save the World from Rampaging Robots • **21:** Dexterity • **41:** Become
a Science Genius • **55:** Break Codes • **79:** Design Your Own Gadgets

Dracula, Count
Carpathian Mountains,
Transylvania

Lecter, Hannibal (Dr.)
Baltimore State Hospital
for the Criminally Insane

No, Julius (Dr.)
Crab Key Island,
Caribbean Sea

Smith, Agent
The Matrix

Vader, Darth
Death Star, Deep Space

Who, Dr.
Somewhere in time

Wicked Witch, The
The Land of Oz
(Western Quarter)

Build a Network of Contacts

No matter how powerful you are, you can't have eyes and ears everywhere unless they're other people's eyes and ears. Nor can you hope to surf different worlds, especially elite or specialized ones, without an invitation. When you're a superhero, it's not what or whom you know—it's both.

Friends and Acquaintances

- Your contacts not only unwittingly keep tabs on the world for you, they are experts you can consult. Design some business cards for yourself. Make up a job like "Researcher"—something vague and not interesting enough to invite curiosity, but one that will give you the opportunity to consult those you meet when you need to.
- Always be on the lookout to meet new people and expand your network. Join clubs and societies and accept all party invitations. You'll have to overcome any shyness if you're to strike up conversations with strangers, but it's an important skill.
- Target people in positions of power or with insider information about what's going on in the community, who's doing what, and how systems work. Don't ask too many questions or make them feel like they're being interrogated, though. Find casual ways of extracting useful info and build up trust, so that when you need a favor, and one with no questions asked, they'll be happy to oblige.
- Put just enough effort in to sustain good relations with new contacts. Memorize any personal details and always send them a holiday card.

Let's talk about you: People love talking about themselves, so when they start asking you too many questions, try to steer the conversation back to them. Show an active interest in them and what they do, and they'll provide all the information you need.

Build a Network of Contacts **Form**

Once you have mastered this **Way to Become a Superhero**,
stick your Achieved Star here and fill in the form

Achieved

CONTACT SHEET

Photocopy this page and use it to keep track of the people you meet who you think could be useful to you in some way. Make a note of how they might come in handy.

Name

Occupation

Contact details

What could they be useful for?

| Whom they know | y/n | Insider information | y/n |
| Power/pulling strings | y/n | Money/ resources | y/n |

Are they good or evil?

Good ☐   Evil ☐   Not sure ☐

Name

Occupation

Contact details

What could they be useful for?

| Whom they know | y/n | Insider information | y/n |
| Power/pulling strings | y/n | Money/ resources | y/n |

Are they good or evil?

Good ☐   Evil ☐   Not sure ☐

Name

Occupation

Contact details

What could they be useful for?

| Whom they know | y/n | Insider information | y/n |
| Power/pulling strings | y/n | Money/ resources | y/n |

Are they good or evil?

Good ☐   Evil ☐   Not sure ☐

NOTES

STAY CONNECTED

Set up a Facebook or a LinkedIn page so you can keep in touch with your contacts and see who else they're connected to.

Did you use this power for...

GOOD? or

☐ *EVIL?*

☐

At the same time you could master these other **Ways**:
40: Understand Body Language • **65**: Talk Your Way Out of Trouble • **72**: Speak a Hundred Languages • **88**: Acquire Specialist Knowledge • **97**: Know What's Happening Everywhere

Lead from the Front

It's a tough gig. You appear out of nowhere, no one knows who you really are, and yet they have to do as you say. At least they do if they want to survive and, in the case of your superteam or the police, catch the bad guys. Many of the vital skills needed as a leader are covered in other sections. Making quick decisions (and the right ones), setting goals, and knowing what you stand for—they all form part of the makeup of a superhero. The trick is to pull them all together.

Follow the Leader

- You may not be a born leader, but that doesn't mean you can't become one. It's not all about being a dominant person. For example, clearly it'd be useful to be a powerful, articulate speaker, but you also need to be a good, patient listener. List the leadership qualities you think you already possess, and then those you lack or that need a lot of development. Focus on the aim of motivating people. This is key. Sometimes shouting, "Do as I say or you're all gonna die!" won't work and more subtle methods may be required.

- Put your leadership skills to the test by setting up a club. Success can be measured by how effectively you attract people to join your club, how you inspire and motivate them to fulfill the aims of the club (which means you must know what they are and communicate them clearly), how you handle any disagreements between members of the club, and how you delegate responsibilities.

 "Keep your fears to yourself, but share your courage with others," said R. L. Stevenson. It's amazing how infectious positivity can be. Your self-belief and conviction will inspire others to fight on even after you've had to depart—an example of leading by example.

Lead from the Front **Form**

Once you have mastered this **Way to Become a Superhero**,
stick your Achieved Star here and fill in the form

☆ **Achieved**

JOIN THE CLUB

How good are you at motivating and organizing people? Set up a club or society and find out. You could use it as a cover for some of your superhero training. Whatever the purpose, be sure to have a constitution in place.

THIS IS THE CONSTITUTION OF

> Club/Society name here

The objective of the club is to . . .

Founder/President:

> Your name here

Secretary:

Treasurer:

How do people become members?

By invitation ☐   By nomination and vote ☐

By application ☐   Anyone can join ☐

Fee/subscription charge (if any) $ 0,0 . 0,0

Description of events/activities:

Venues/equipment required:

CLUB RULES

Members found in breach of these rules may be stripped of club membership

After six months of running the club, complete the following leadership review:

No. of members   0,0

No. of disputes between members   0,0

No. of events held   0,0

Rate the popularity of your club   out of 10

Have all these disputes been resolved?   y/n

Rate the success of these events   out of 10

Overall leadership rating   out of 10

At the same time you could master these other **Ways:**
9: Select a Sidekick • **20**: Learn to Multitask • **46**: Choose a Cause • **78**: Be a Good Influence • **93**: Develop Powers of Persuasion • **99**: Gather a Superteam

Know What's Happening Everywhere

Current affairs is one area of knowledge it is vital that you apply yourself to. If you don't know what's going on in the world, you won't be in a position to foresee potential problems, handle tricky situations with diplomacy, and know which resources can be relied on and which can't.

News Views

- Regularly read a cross-section of newspapers and news websites, skimming the headlines for events that require your special attention. Avoid getting involved, if you can, in any political hot potatoes.
- Check out smaller, more local stories to catch potential problems at their grass roots and investigate any quirky or unexplained stories that might suggest a powerfully devious hand at work. Don't waste your time on big projects that have the attention of everyone—politicians, military, and police. Your work should be of a more undercover nature.
- Read the comment sections so that you can gauge public opinion. Evil geniuses love to manipulate people in order to gain power. You need to have a finger on the pulse to detect danger signals.
- Monitor major cities, as criminal masterminds don't like to be sideshows and if they're planning something dastardly they'll be after maximum impact. But keep an eye on the quietest places on Earth too, as they make great locations for secret bases and hideouts.
- Keep on top of the latest environmental reports and monitor the weather systems, so that you can anticipate any natural disasters.

> **Superczars:** Don't forget to read celebrity magazines and follow the latest gossip. Evil geniuses are attracted to the rich and famous, usually because they want a piece of the cake themselves. Make a list of celebrities with a shadier side and monitor their activities.

Know What's Happening
Everywhere **Form**

Once you have mastered this **Way to Become a Superhero**,
stick your Achieved Star here and fill in the form

Achieved

READ ALL ABOUT IT

Scan the papers looking for a story that suggests an evil genius's hand at work.
Make a note of the important details of the newsworthy event that might offer
clues leading to the capture of your supervillain.

Stick your story's headline here

Date and time of event

m m d d y y y y   :

Location

What is it about this story that arouses your suspicions?

Could it be part of
some bigger plot? y/n

If yes, what do you
think that plot is?

Who are your three main suspects?

Does this story
warrant further
investigation? y/n

Fold and stick any related articles here

Did you use
this power
for...
GOOD? or
□
EVIL?
□

At the same time you could master these other **Ways**:
10: Stealth • **16**: Sixth Sense • **27**: See in the Dark • **36**: Be in Two Places at Once
43: Invisibility • **77**: X-Ray Vision • **80**: Orientation • **95**: Build a Network of Contacts

Swim Like a Fish

Unless you've decided that a fear of water is to be your critical weak spot (see **Way to Become a Superhero** No. 26), it is vital that you know how to swim, and not only that, but swim like you were born in the water.

Sink or Swim

- Find your local swimming pool. If you haven't already, you need to master some of the key swimming styles. The front crawl (or "freestyle") is best for speed, but over long distances you may need to mix it with the backstroke (with scissor kicks instead of flutter kicks) and something that gives you more of a rest between strokes, like breaststroke or sidestroke. Also learn to tread water.
- The key to fast and efficient swimming is to establish a smooth, regular rhythm to your breathing that doesn't interfere with your strokes, so honing your breathing technique is vital. Practice breathing in through your mouth (which you would obviously do above water) and out through your nose (which you can do underwater). It's important to be able to swim underwater too, so practice deep breathing and holding your breath, and take diving lessons. Yoga can help you to make full use of your lung capacity.
- Once you've mastered your swimming styles, do a lifesaving course— after all, that's what being a superhero is all about. The course will give you the vital experience of swimming in clothes, which is hard work. A cape might be pushing it though, so make sure yours is detachable!

 Get the drift: Hero or villain, one of the other vital aquatic skills you should acquire is floating. This will help you if you ever need to play dead in the water as a way of escape, or if you are cast adrift at sea for long periods and need to conserve energy.

Swim Like a Fish **Form**

Once you have mastered this **Way to Become a Superhero**, stick your Achieved Star here and fill in the form

Achieved

DUCKING AND DIVING

Improving your swimming skills doesn't have to be all work and no play. Here are three swimming-pool games that will put your aquabatics to the test—do seek permission from the pool owners before playing them. You and your friends all need to be competent swimmers for these games, but only one of you should be a superswimmer . . .

Game 1—Shark Attack
No. of players: 3 +

Object of game: to escape the jaws of the shark • **Skills:** speed and agility in the water

Everyone starts in one corner of the shallow end. The person who is nominated to play the shark stays there and counts to 20 while everyone else swims away to deeper waters. On reaching 20, the shark sets off in pursuit of his/her victims. Once a victim is "eaten" (i.e., caught) they must return to the corner of the shallow end and wait there until the game is over. The winner (i.e., you) is the person who escapes the shark's jaws for longest. It's good practice for you to play the shark in this game too. You can all take turns.

How many games did you play? `0 , 0`

How many times did you win by outlasting all the other swimmers? `0 , 0`

As shark, how long did it take you to "eat" all your victims?

`0 , 0` mins `0 , 0` secs

Game 2—Aqua-Man Says
No. of players: 3 +

Object of game: to listen carefully to instructions and perform swimming skills • **Skills:** floating, swimming, diving—a bit of everything!

This is based on the game "Simon Says." Pick a player to be Aqua-Man. He or she must shout out instructions to the other players to perform various swimming skills (e.g., floating on your back, doing an underwater somersault, swimming to the end of the pool and back, holding your breath underwater, treading water, etc.). The other players must obey only if the instructions begin with the words "Aqua-Man says . . ." If Aqua-Man gives a command without saying this and a player still obeys, then that player is out. Players can also be out for being the slowest to perform an "Aqua-Man says" instruction, or for failing to follow an instruction correctly. The last player left (i.e., you) is the winner. Take turns being Aqua-Man.

How many games did you play? `0 , 0`

How many times did you win by outlasting all the other swimmers? `0 , 0`

What was the hardest instruction you were given?

[ ]

Game 3—Treasure Hunt
No. of players: 3 +

Object of game: to recover as much hidden treasure as possible • **Skills:** diving and swimming underwater

Nominate someone to be the Pirate Captain. He/she must "bury" (i.e., toss into the water) various objects that will sink to the bottom of the pool, such as coins, pebbles, spoons, etc. The other players must turn away while this happens. On the Pirate Captain's command (a whistle), everyone jumps in and starts searching for the objects. Each object collected is worth 1 point, with one of the objects being especially valuable and worth a bounty of 5 points. The Pirate Captain should give another whistle after three minutes to mark the end of the hunt. The person with the greatest number of points once the treasure has all been counted is the winner.

How many games did you play? `0 , 0`

How many times did you win? `0 , 0`

Did you use this power for . . . **GOOD?** [ ] *or* **EVIL?** [ ]

At the same time you could master these other **Ways:**
3: Take Flight • **10:** Stealth • **13:** Conquer Your Fears • **58:** Withstand Heat and Cold
76: Devise an Escape Plan

Gather a Superteam

If you've tackled **Ways to Become a Superhero** Nos. 9 and 37, you'll have a sidekick and superpet trained and ready to leap into action with you. Sometimes, though, an evil genius will gather armies of henchmen and plan something so global and so devious it takes more than one superhero to fight the good fight. When the going gets rough, and you need some assistance, who you gonna call?

Supertroopers

- Look in your superhero address book. What other superheroes do you know? Perhaps you've met some at a summit or social event, or you've happened to turn up at the same world-saving mission. Make a list of those you think you could work well with. Avoid any huge egos. This is still your gig, and there can only be one team leader.
- When selecting possible members for your superteam, you need to think not only about whom you can actually get along with, but what skills they will bring to the table. A veritable smorgasbord of superpowers will mean you are ready to face any kind of challenge, physical or mental. Try to plug the gaps in your own set of skills.
- Arrange a team-building day. Do some activities to build up trust, test fitness, and get your superhero pals solving problems together. These games will also help you assess the level of their skills. Give yourselves a team name and decide among you how to divide up superheroic responsibilities.

Friends anonymous: It's not easy meeting like-minded superheroes, as they tend to be a secretive bunch. But if anyone's going to be able to identify the telltale signs of someone with a double life, it's you—start by looking for a copy of this book stashed among their things.

Gather a Superteam **Form**

Once you have mastered this **Way to Become a Superhero**, stick your Achieved Star here and fill in the form

☆ Achieved

MY SUPERTEAM

Write the name of your superteam here

Name

Place a photo of superteam member 1 here

VITAL STATISTICS

Strengths

Weaknesses

Responsibilities

Reliability rating   10

Team-player rating   10

Name

Place a photo of superteam member 2 here

VITAL STATISTICS

Strengths

Weaknesses

Responsibilities

Reliability rating   10

Team-player rating   10

Name

Place a photo of superteam member 3 here

VITAL STATISTICS

Strengths

Weaknesses

Responsibilities

Reliability rating   10

Team-player rating   10

Name

Place a photo of your sidekick here

VITAL STATISTICS

Strengths

Weaknesses

Responsibilities

Reliability rating   10

Team-player rating   10

Name

Place a photo of your superpet here

VITAL STATISTICS

Strengths

Weaknesses

Responsibilities

Reliability rating   10

Team-player rating   10

Did you use this power for... **GOOD?** or ☐ **EVIL?** ☐

At the same time you could master these other **Ways**:
9: Select a Sidekick • **23**: Plan for World Domination • **37**: Train Your Superpet
93: Develop Powers of Persuasion • **96**: Lead from the Front

I'll be back . . .

(when you least expect it)

Devise Your Villainous Comeback

If at first you don't succeed, you know what to do. You can be very trying, and that's a good thing, because nobody respects a quitter. What doesn't kill you makes you stronger, and that's the best thing about a comeback. In round two your nemesis will be the same person they were before, if not weaker from all their efforts in round one. You, however, will be better equipped, better prepared, and more evil than ever.

Down, But Not Out

- While you're taking time out in hiding, assessing the damage from your last campaign and consolidating your forces, take an honest look at how things went so badly wrong. Some of the blame will lie with your minions—eliminate these weaknesses in your workforce—but there'll have been flaws in your master plan too. What have you learned about your enemies that might be used against them next time around?
- Put world domination plans aside for now and devote your efforts to revenge. Before you can get back on course you need to squish the fly in your ointment, crush the wrench in your works, and extract the thorn in your side. Use all your guile and brilliant wit to create an elaborate trap, and once you've lured your nemesis in, allow yourself time to gloat in their face before pulling the plug. Muahaha!
- A comeback is an opportunity to reinvent yourself. A new identity can be refreshing and provides a way back into the underworld you used to inhabit as well as a chance to get close to your enemies undetected.

I'll be back . . . as your governor: When it comes to comebacks, nobody is more iconic than Arnold Schwarzenegger as the Terminator. His saying "I'll be back" not only spurred sequels, it also became true when he reinvented himself as the governor of California in 2003.

Devise Your Villainous Comeback **Form**

Once you have mastered this **Way to Become an Evil Genius**,
stick your Achieved Star here and fill in the form

Achieved

━━━ REVENGE IS A DISH BEST SERVED COLD ━━━

Get inventive in the kitchen of villainy and come up with a dish that will satisfy your appetite for
revenge and show your enemies who the true master chef is around here.

INGREDIENTS

What goes into your revenge dish? List what
you need (e.g., people, equipment) below

1

2

3

4

5

6

STEP-BY-STEP INSTRUCTIONS

How will you make your superhero nemesis
and the world pay dearly for crossing you?

Step 1

Step 2

Step 3

Step 4

Step 5

Step 6

Chill overnight before serving.

━━━━━━━━━ REVENGE IS SWEET ━━━━━━━━━

Think back to the last time you took revenge on an enemy.

What did they do to you?

How did you get them back?

| How did revenge taste? | Very sweet ☐ | Pretty sweet ☐ |
| Bland ☐ | A bit bitter ☐ | Sour ☐ |

Are you now caught in a vicious cycle of revenge? ☐ y/n

Who is winning? You ☐   Your enemy ☐

At the same time you could master these other **Ways**:
23: Plan for World Domination • **33**: Anticipate Your Enemy's Next Move • **38**: Assemble
Your Armies of Darkness • **53**: Be Ruthless • **56**: Invent Some Great One-Liners

Save the World from Yourself

You can tell yourself there's no way you'd ever allow powers of evil to overcome you and control you, but if it can happen to Superman, Spider-Man, and a host of others, then there's every chance that you too could find yourself in that same dark place. It's important to recognize the warning signs so that you can fight back.

Dear Diary, Today I Tried to Destroy the World . . .

- Be the master of your powers; don't let them be the master of you. If you feel at all intoxicated by your own greatness or infected by your bad experiences, get yourself to a monastery to learn some humility.
- Design some booby traps around your bedroom to ensure you'll wake up at the slightest sign of danger. Superheroes are as vulnerable as anyone else when unconscious, which means bedtime is when you're most at risk of being poisoned or subjected to the mind-control techniques of your enemies. Never let your guard down.
- When you're not yourself, you'll need your trusted sidekick to remind you who you really are. This is a big favor because, most likely, you won't want to hear it. Choose a mantra or some form of visual stimulus you can refer to daily to focus your mind on your true mission. Your sidekick can use it to help pull you back from the brink of the abyss.
- If you're lucky enough to realize when you're out of control, the best thing you can do is to put yourself out of action. Destroy your suit and lock yourself away until you learn to defeat the enemy within.

Born again: In a rare moment of clarity, Jean Grey (one of the X-Men) made the ultimate sacrifice and ended her own life to put down the Dark Phoenix she had become. This drastic action isn't recommended unless, like her, you can guarantee coming back to life.

Save the World . . .
from Yourself **Form**

Once you have mastered this **Way to Become a Superhero**,
stick your Achieved Star here and fill in the form

☆ **Achieved**

YOURSELF
—— KNOW YOUR ENEMY ——

Are you concerned that you might be becoming your own worst enemy? Spot the signs of an identity crisis early and take appropriate measures.

Which of these do you recognize in yourself?   Your weaknesses

Short temper ☐   Nemesis envy ☐

Killing sprees ☐   Selfish behavior ☐

Your strengths

Refusal to listen ☐   A wild look in the eyes ☐

On a scale of 0–10, how angry are you feeling? [10]

What is causing this anger?

Troubling dreams/visions ☐   An evil voice in my head ☐

A tragic event in my past ☐   The pressure of a double life ☐

My inability to express myself ☐   I wish I knew ☐

YOU NEED A PLAN OF ACTION. WILL YOU . . .		Explain how you will carry out your plan below
. . . increase your defenses?	y/n	
. . . confide in a loved one?	y/n	
. . . destroy your superhero suit?	y/n	
. . . ask your sidekick to lock you away?	y/n	
. . . go to counseling?	y/n	

Place a photo of you looking deranged here

Did you use this power for . . .
GOOD? or
☐ EVIL?
☐

At the same time you could master these other **Ways**:
1: Discover Your Alter Ego • **12**: Mind Control • **25**: Control Your Temper • **26**: Know Your Weaknesses • **54**: Make Sacrifices • **73**: Create a Force Field • **84**: Resist Temptation

Appendix

In the following pages are items to help you get more out of your
101 Ways to Become a Superhero . . . Or an Evil Genius book

Your **Ways to Become a Superhero**

A list for you to fill in with any **Ways to Become a Superhero** that
weren't mentioned in the book but that you think should be included.

Answers

After you've attempted the tricky quizzes, riddles, and mazes, see if
you got the answers right. Hey! No cheating.

Pocket-Sized Checklist

A handy checklist to keep with you all the time. You can use it to
remind yourself daily of your superhuman endeavors and to check off
the **Ways to Become a Superhero** the minute you've completed
them.

Extra Paper

Photocopy the extra pages if you run out of space on a form, and
use them to continue writing. When you're done, attach them to the
relevant form.

Thank Yous

A thank you to all the superheroes and evil geniuses who have helped
to make this book possible.

Identity

Who are we and what do we do?

Stickers!

Once you've completed a super **Way to Become a Superhero** stick
a star over the "Achieved" star on the form.

Your Ways to Become a Superhero

List the **Ways to Become a Superhero** that you'd
like to do that weren't mentioned in the book

Way to Become a Superhero 1

Way to Become a Superhero 2

Way to Become a Superhero 3

Way to Become a Superhero 4

Way to Become a Superhero 5

Way to Become a Superhero 6

Way to Become a Superhero 7

Way to Become a Superhero 8

Way to Become a Superhero 9

Way to Become a Superhero 10

Answers

Hey! No cheating!

WAY TO BECOME A SUPERHERO NO. 7
DECIPHER DEVIOUS RIDDLES

1. Spider-Man

2. X-ray glasses

3. Your nemesis

4. Fingerprints

WAY TO BECOME A SUPERHERO NO. 20
LEARN TO MULTITASK
DOUBLE TROUBLE – ROUND 1:

1. **9**

2. **21**

3. **8**

4. **12**

5. **50**

NAME SPUR = **SUPERMAN**
NOW WE RANDOM = **WONDER WOMAN**
NEW OR EVIL = **WOLVERINE**
DEAD LIVER = **DAREDEVIL**
TOM ODOR COD = **DOCTOR DOOM**

DOUBLE TROUBLE – ROUND 2:

1. **6**

2. **7**

3. **13**

4. **30**

5. **13**

DREAM SPIN = **SPIDER-MAN**
BANTAM = **BATMAN**
A MAC TOWN = **CATWOMAN**
NOBLE GINGER = **GREEN GOBLIN**
A TRAFFIC SNOUT = **FANTASTIC FOUR**

WAY TO BECOME A SUPERHERO NO. 29
SOLVE IMPOSSIBLE PROBLEMS
BRAIN TRAIN:

1. **18**

2. i. **60 Seconds in a Minute**
ii. **12 Days of Christmas**
iii. **101 Ways to Become a Superhero**
iv. **3 Blind Mice (See How They Run)**

3. **46**

4. **iii**

5. **10**

6. **2 – the number of letters in the alphabet between V and Y.**

7. **Just about. It will take you 48 mins to get home (time = distance/speed) and if you leak a gallon every 16 mins, you'll lose 3 gallons over the journey (48/16), leaving you with 4 gallons of fuel to get home on. Four gallons will take you 100 mi (4 x 25)—exactly the length of your journey.**

WAY TO BECOME A SUPERHERO NO. 55
BREAK CODES
DECODE:

UNLOCK THIS CODE USING THE KEY BELOW

WAY TO BECOME A SUPERHERO NO. 58
WITHSTAND HEAT AND COLD

1. **32** / 2. **98.6** / 3. **9** / 4. **-459.4** / 5. **-128.2** / 6. **Vostok, Antarctica** / 7. **-454** / 8. **212** / 9. **21,632** / 10. **Lightning bolt** – Surface of the sun's top temperature (approx): 9,941°F. Lightning bolt's top temperature (approx): 54,032°F / 11. **136.4°** / 12. **El Azizia, Libya**

Answers

Hey! No cheating!

WAY TO BECOME A SUPERHERO NO. 63
OBSERVATION SKILLS
SPOT THE DIFFERENCE

IN PICTURE TWO . . .
1. . . . the middle line coming from the
telephone receiver in the call signal is missing
2. . . . the Empire State Building
(second left) is shorter
3. . . . the swinging superhero's rope is shorter
4. . . . the arch on the front of the
central building is fatter
5. . . . the third UFO is missing a shaft of light
6. . . . one of the lightning strikes is longer

WAY TO BECOME AN EVIL GENIUS NO. 76
DEVISE AN ESCAPE PLAN

WAY TO BECOME A SUPERHERO NO. 80
ORIENTATION

Building 1 is **Empire State
Building, NY, USA**

Building 2 is **Eiffel Tower,
Paris, France**

Building 3 is **Sydney Opera
House, Australia**

Skyline 1 is **Hong Kong**

Skyline 2 is **New York**

Outline 1 is **Peru**

Outline 2 is **Afghanistan**

Outline 3 is **New Zealand**

WAY TO BECOME A SUPERHERO NO. 90
HEALING

1. b

2. a—wrapping the wound in something non-
fluffy like plastic wrap or a plastic bag will keep
the wound clean. Remember to remove any
items of jewelry in case of swelling.

3. d—if this still doesn't remove the obstruction,
you could try giving the victim five upward
abdominal thrusts, but you'll need proper
training to learn how to do this safely.

4. a—quiet casualties may be unconscious and
have stopped breathing. They should therefore
be first priority.

5. c—if you cannot turn the current off at the
source, push the source of electricity away from
the victim with a nonconductive object, such as
a dry wooden stick or rolled-up newspaper.

6. b

7. c—after removing the sting this way, raise the
affected limb above the level of the victim's heart
and apply a cold compress to reduce swelling.

8. b—call an ambulance and help the victim
to sit down with their knees bent and leaning
forward at about 75 degrees. If they're over 16
and there's no reason not to, you can give them
an aspirin (not acetaminophen) to chew to help
avoid blood clotting.

How to Use Your Pocket-Sized Checklist

Use the following instructions to keep track of the superhuman
Ways to Become a Superhero you've mastered at a moment's notice.

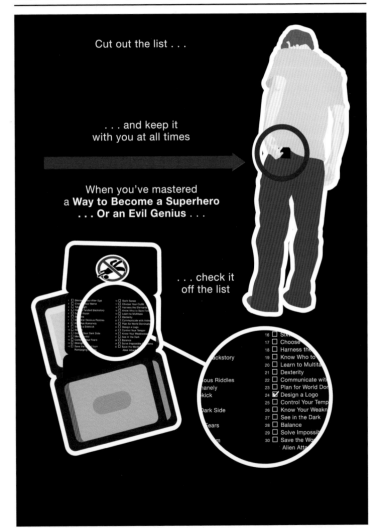

Thank Yous and Noteworthy Acknowledgments

Write your own acknowledgments
over the example below

The authors wish to thank:

George **"Vice Verser"** Szirtes for devising devious riddles
for **Way to Become a Superhero** No. 7

Philippa Milnes-Smith, aka **"Agent Smith"**

Ed **"Sanchoplanbot"** Cookson, Tim **"Dialectrix"** Moss,
Dave Varela aka **"Varelatron,"** Robert **"Bobby Fire"** Ellis
& Jane **"Brain Storm"** Horne for contributing superideas

Ele **"The Commissioner"** Fountain, Margaret **"Magic
Pen"** Histed, Katherine **"Productron"** Grimes, Susannah
"Nuke 'Em" Nuckey, Emma **"Publicitus"** Bradshaw,
Kevin **"The Silent Assassin"** Perry, Stacy Cantor, Malte
Ritter, Hermann Zanier—key members of **T.U.M.S. (The
Ultimate Mega-Superteam)**

Clarissa **"Artemis Craft"** Upchurch, Tom **"Shur-i-kan"**
Szirtes, Christine **"Greenfingers"** Horne & Neville
"Lightfoot" Horne for providing superteam support

Identity

About the Authors

Richard Horne (aka **One-o-one-o-tron**) was born into a universe of chaos . . . Only by unleashing his list-making abilities could he impose his vision of order on an uncompiled world. His master plan has secretly been set out in the bestselling manuals *101 Things to Do Before You Die, 101 Things to Do Before You're Old and Boring, 101 Things You Need to Know . . . and Some You Don't*, and *101 Things You Wish You'd Invented . . . and Some You Wish No One Had*, and in the ultimate handbook of doom, *A Is for Armageddon*. His dark arts can also be found in *How to Survive a Robot Uprising, Where's My Jetpack?, How to Build a Robot Army*, and *The Dangerous Book for Boys*.

ONE-O-ONE-O-TRON

VITAL STATISTICS
Status: EVIL GENIUS
Special power: DARK ARTS
Fighting style: NORTHERN STREET STYLE
Weapons: WORDS & PICTURES
Weakness: HELVETICA

Originally from somewhere else, **Helen Szirtes** (aka **The Scribbler**) found herself marooned on Earth after an unusually heavy meteor shower. Using her feline instincts, Venusian xylophone, and synesthetic powers, she managed to integrate into human society, where she found acceptance in spite of her involuntary doodling, electronic beeping, and sporadic versifying. In 2005, she coauthored *101 Things to Do Before You're Old and Boring*. She thought writing this book would put people off the scent of her secret identity with a cunning double bluff. She was wrong.

THE SCRIBBLER

VITAL STATISTICS
Status: SUPERHERO
Special power: SYNESTHESIA
Fighting style: JAZZ FUSION
Weapons: MULTICOLORED PEN
Weakness: HUNGARIAN PAPRIKA